MEMOIR OF A GHETTO BASTARD

BY
WILLIAM "UNIQUE" BATTLE

Transcribed by
Terri Greene & Melissa Sue Griffith
Edited by
Travelin' Light Publishing

Copyrights ©2021 William Battle Memoir of a Ghetto Bastard is a work of creative non-fiction. The events in this memoir are true to the best of the author's memory. Some names and identifying features have been changed to protect the identity of certain parties. The author in no way represents any company, corporation, or brand, mentioned herein.

Published by Travelin' Light Publishing, LLC

Email:travelinlight.mg@gmail.com

www.travelinlightpublishing.com

ISBN:9780578943565

PROLOGUE

It started somewhere in a jailhouse over fifty years ago where my uncle was serving time for a bank robbery. I heard he had a couple of pictures of my mother sitting on his locker and a man that he was talking to on the gate inquired about a picture of her. His name was William Duncan who was also serving time for bank robbery. Somehow, William Duncan convinces my uncle whose name was Mousey to introduce him to my mother. In this case he did. I don't know the facts on how it all materialized but nonetheless, upon William Duncan's release he and my mother got together. The unique hook up, if I should say so.

September 18, 1969, I was born. I have no idea of how long their relationship lasted but it wasn't long. I remember my father being in my life vividly, not too clearly. I just heard stories about his pimping and robbing. My mother said my father was extremely jealous and that his jealousy would later end their relationship. As I grew older, I've seen different. I learned my mother was quite promiscuous and attracted to younger men. She fixed my mind on such thoughts like, my father used to spy on her from rooftops and things of that nature. But I learned there's two sides to every story and Mother was not an angel. I do remember my father going back to prison again for a bank robbery and my mother taking me to see him. He was behind a glass window, and I had to speak to him through a phone, but we couldn't touch. He used to write me letters and draw pictures. I attribute my writing and drawing skills to his because over the years, I became fond of writing and drawing. Anyway, My Mom stopped communicating with him so that was the end of me and my pop's relationship until he was released years later. Mom had moved on, in and out of different relationships which none lasted. Over the time I became a mother's boy like most young men because there's no father image in their lives. I must admit my mother did everything in her power to provide for me and my older brother. With the help of my Grandparents, we always had food, clothing and shelter. My Grandparents were working class people. My grandmother worked in a factory and my grandfather who I later discovered was my step- grandfather was a Veteran. He fought in the Korean War in the Navy, then later became a truck driver for Domino Sugar Company. They were family-oriented, they stuck together and helped each other. At least that's how it appeared to me but, I later discover different.

CHAPTER ONE
THE AFTER HOURS JOINT

My Grandparents were the neighborhood bootleggers. They had a bar in the basement which was an after-hours spot where they sold bottles of liquor. There was always friends and family over. I mean at least twenty to thirty people in the basement every night. My Mother would bring me and my older brother with her to the basement because she and my cousin Connie who was her partner in crime served the drinks and played the music. I must admit my Mom and Connie were some fine sexy women. So sexy and fine that they later caught the attention of Royce and Danny Lawless. Royce was a smooth diamond wearing cat who wore tailor made suits and Gator shoes. Danny Lawless was older than Royce and was a tough breed type of gangster who owned a lot of the neighborhood businesses. One was a Diner where all the gangsters hung out including Royce.

Back then the neighborhood of Bushwick was owned by the Italians and the blacks ran the businesses for them but not Danny and Royce. Royce owned a record shop and a few other businesses. But nevertheless, Royce and my mother hooked up as well as Connie and Danny.

I remember the first time they went on a date. My mother was in the house getting dressed and playing her oldies. I had never seen her this happy. She dressed me and my brother and walked us over to my Grandparents house. Me and my brother went into the bar to get pickled pig feet from the jar. Mom and Connie went off to the side and slapped each other five and they started whispering. Connie put on one of those oldies and my Grandmother started dancing and grabbing my Grandfather to dance with her, but he refused. Suddenly in walks in this cat with a Stetson hat, sleek pants, gator shoes and a leather blazer jacket. He had on a diamond pinky ring and wore nice smelling cologne. He presented the presence of what I later learned was the characteristics of what a man of power displayed. At first, I didn't like the fact that my Mother was giving this man more attention than I. Like I said, I was a mama's boy.

I walked over to my Mom while they were talking and stepped between them. Royce laughed and said, "what's up little man?" I didn't respond to him.

Instead, I tried to pull my Mother away. Then my Grandmother came over and said, "Boogaloo don't nobody want your Momma but you." She winked at Royce, then gave me a bag of potato chips to distract me but it didn't work. I grabbed my Mother's hand again. Royce then walked outside and sat in his brown Cadillac. When my Mother went out to meet him, I followed. When I reached outside, Royce called me over to his car and said, "what's your problem you don't like me? Maybe you'll like this car." He opened the door and sat me inside the car on his lap, he put the keys in and said pull off. I was amazed. I never pulled off but, he allowed me to play with the radio and wear his pinky ring while in the car. He opened the glove compartment and gave me a bag of Mary Jane and squirrel nut candies. Then he gave me a five-dollar bill and said, "now let me take your Mommy for a ride." I then told my Mom I would see her later. She laughed and said, "boy you are a sellout!" Connie slapped me in the back of the head and said get your ass in the basement and I went running.

The next morning Royce came to my Grandma's house to take me and my brother to eat lunch. I did notice how Royce dug me more than my brother. As we ate, he would say slick sayings like "man up little nigger! I'm going to make you a man!" Anyway, as time went on Royce begin molding me. He allowed me to work in his candy store, his liquor store and even let me hang out in his record shop. Man, I'd seen him call shots, I'd seen him count money, I'd even seen him knock out three brothers. The McClam brothers who were infamous bullies and stick-up kids. Everything Royce did I tried to mimic. He was my idol and every move I made was me acting like him. Every word I uttered, were words I heard him speak.

I remember one day I saw him make some type of deal with some people and he paid a guy to drop it off. I said, "you don't have to pay him I'll do it." He laughed and patted me on the head. Later that week he gave me a list

of names and told me to drop some papers off to all the addresses and names on the list. Royce saw my hustle and established a newspaper run for me. Just thinking of this brings tears to my eyes. How a man who wasn't my real pops believed in me. He always told me to finish school and stay out of the streets. He said if I finished school, he would buy me my first car. I swear this man was the epitome of a man. I began to get noticed by number runners, dope dealers, dope fiends, pimps and gamblers. I mean everybody loved me. I was Royce's little Son. Everywhere I went they would say "hey little Boogaloo!" Then they'd whisper,
"that's Royce's little boy!"
It was at the point of my life where I started to realize how one's self-esteem could be lifted. I was in the middle of power and respect and boy did I feel good! Mom seemed happy, everything was fine and dandy.
Life was a three-ring circus.
One day Royce came over with a gift for me. He had brought me two pair of boxing gloves. One was an eight-ounce pair and the other was a sixteen ounce. He told me I was to wear the eight-ounce gloves and let

Everyday uncle Steve was back in the window screaming, "didn't I say stick and move!" Then one day he came downstairs and put the gloves on with me and started showing me the fundamentals of boxing. He began to train me every day and I was becoming good at it. By then my Grandfather started standing on the back porch watching me. One night the boxer Michael Moore's father came around. He saw me in action and said that I was good, but I needed more training. My grandfather was beside himself drinking and started his mess about me beating any kid in the neighborhood. The very next night my Grandparents had one of their get-togethers and all the old cats had me in the backyard square off with some other kid. Until today I have no idea who the kid was and assumed it was one of my Grandfather's friend's kid. I hope it was Michael Moore because I whipped his ass. Michael Moore went on to become the heavyweight champ of the world. I also fought Junior Jones before he went to become a world champion. Now I have hustling skills plus fighting skills and I'm creating my own character. The makings of a little Royce were in effect.

whoever my opponent was to wear the sixteen-ounce gloves. He explained to me that the sixteen-ounce gloves were heavier and would make my opponents slower and the eight-ounce gloves were lighter which would make me faster. Back then other than Royce, my other Idol was Muhammad Ali. I tried to emulate him to the fullest like every little black kid in the seventies.

One Christmas Royce brought me a Muhammad Ali and Joe Frazier boxing toy. I loved that toy and you couldn't pull me away from it. Everywhere I went I had to take my boxing gloves along especially to my Grandparent's house which was down the block. Back then we lived in a great big apartment building at 157 Cooper Street and my Grandparents lived at 188 Cooper Street. I would go to the backyard and practice all day. Steven and Bertha, who I called aunt and uncle were close friends to my Grandparents. Uncle Steve used to work for MLB as an enforcer for a trucking company in Midtown Manhattan. He used to watch me from the window and scream "bob and weave! Stick and move Boogaloo! Boxing is a dance boy, so dance!"

called him the man. Then I started seeing movies like The Mac and Superfly and damn if Royce wasn't the man and I was his son. It's often said that your circumstances and your environment shapes and molds your present and future situation. I'm a firm believer in such cliches and sayings. For example, if you're raised in an aggressive environment, nine out of ten times it probably will make you aggressive. However, it can also have an adverse effect on you. But this wasn't the case with me, I was just a very observant kid. I learned at an early age how to be a fox and a lion when required or necessary. I was a man-child and everyday became a learning experience for me. I was inquisitive and my brain was symbolic to a sponge. As time progressed, I started venturing off on my own. Although I was Royce's son, I wanted my own identity, so I started mangling with peers of my own. I had intentions of constructing my own outfit/team and I intended to do so by all means. In the process I made a lot of errors. I couldn't tell Royce what I was attempting because he was trying to make a model person out of me. You know how family or parents say, "don't do as I do, do as I say." It certainly isn't that simple especially when you admire

One day while working in the record store, a man walks in with my mother and point to me. To no surprise it's my biological Father and I don't remember him. Royce tells me, "Hey boy that's your father! Go on and say hello." I refused. Royce walked me outside and I take off running. My biological pops and my mom gave chase. I must be honest; I was upset and didn't understand why he came around now. What was his intentions? What was my mother trying to prove? By all means, Royce was my pops. Why did my Mother bring this man to my father's record shop with this BS? Royce came around the corner and walked me up the block and said to me "that's your Father, I'm your Pops. Then he sat me down and explained to me that any nigger could be a father but only a man could be a dad. Then he said, for me to go see what he had to say. To be honest, I couldn't tell you what he said because Royce was my Pops.

Anyway, by now my Mother is carrying Royce's baby and I'm starting to see Royce as what people in the hood back then would call "the man." Everybody is saying, "Annie Jean is carrying a baby for the man!" I'm like what do they mean the man? Years later Royce told me why they what you're seeing. I started out hustling legitimately. I began selling newspapers and giving them to other kids in the neighborhood like John Edwards and little Ricky. John Edwards was Reese's son. Reese was a fine ass woman from Panama. Ricky was the son of a lady named Missy. Me and Ricky were similar in characteristics. Ricky's father was a stick-up kid name Joe. In fact, the first time I saw somebody get shot, Ricky's Pop's did it. I can still remember the day clearly. Joe was wearing a beaver hat, sharkskin pant, slick shirt and a pair of mustard Gators. The guy he shot was Willie McClam. I remember him saying, "Willie you need to do your homework before you start running your mouth. Now I rather be cool my brother but if I ever hear you disrespect my wife again, I'm going to lay you where you stand!" Willie said, "I'll beat the shit out of your wimp ass Joe." Joe was around five feet five inches tall. Mr. Joe laughed, looked at me and Ricky and squeezed the trigger and Willie dropped to the pavement. That day I made Ricky my right-hand man. John was smoother and more so covered by his mom. Anyway, me and the fellas were on our way to become who we thought we were to become. Me not knowing, I had already taken the position of a leader, dictator, and a boss man. We had several different rackets. We packed bags at Key Food supermarket, we did squeegee and pumped gas. At first it was just the three of us until I came up with the idea of bringing all the kids on the block with us. See there were at least four different lanes at each gas station, and the supermarket as well. So, I oversaw the guys who were pumping gas and squeegee. John was my assistant and Ricky controlled the supermarket guys. When we finished our day, we would end up in the basement of my Grandparent's house to divide our daily earnings. Me and Ricky would sit behind the bar to count the money and place it in an empty pig feet jar. We repeated the same routine until the end of the week then we'd divide the money up. We would then give it to John, and he would pay the other guys. Now that I'm older I now realize how organized we were at an early age. We were moving like corporate executives without even knowing so.

There's a saying that poverty promotes crime. Which can be true in some instances based on situations/circumstances or even mindset. Poverty also has an adverse effect. It can also create great minds, opportunity, agendas and a sense of purpose. It had a way of making me and my team want more out of life productively. Remember before the crack era a lot of us in the hood desired to be businessmen. A lot of our parents were Five percenters. "Before we became sinners, we had a sense of purpose." A line stolen from a great Poet and rapper. His name is Nas a rapper from Queens.

But nevertheless, at an early age we understood image was everything. Like I said, men like Royce and Ricky's Pops were men who the hood will be deemed as men of power. No matter the situation, they found a way to stand undaunted and resolute in their stance. Whatever adversity they went through it only strengthened their resolve. At least that's how it appeared in the public eye, and we gathered the same mindset. Under the tender age of ten, we moved like men the age of thirty. That right there put us under the scope of all the number runners, pimps and hustlers. Now at every neighborhood card game or dice game we were the talk of the neighborhood.

One day I'm in the barbershop with my mother on Knickerbocker Avenue waiting to get my haircut. Two men were sitting in chairs getting haircuts. One of the men say to the Barber "have you heard about Royce's boy and his crew?" The other man says, "that damn Boogaloo got his shit together!" My mom turns to me, and I look back at her like they're not talking about me. She walks up to the barber chair and ask the man what was he talking about? She told him she was Royce's woman, and I was Boogaloo. The guys in the shop all stop doing whatever it was they were doing and started slapping me five. My mother backed up, put her hand on her hip and shook her head. She sat down and just listened to the questions which were being asked by the guys inquiring about why and how I did what I did. This in turn only made my chest stick out more. Mind you at this point I was yet to venture into any illegal activities, so I was proud of my ambitions. I went on to aspire to be a boss because of how the guys in the barbershop spoke of me. How I organized a corporation type of team and for the next couple of years I didn't have to pay for a haircut. Me, nor Ricky or John. Me personally, started hanging out in the barbershop just to listen to all the hustler, pimps and players. So naturally I started picking up the characteristics of them as well.

Again, I'm only about eleven years old at this point so my style and persona are starting to materialize. Now I walk like a pimp, talk like a player, and dictate like a hustler. Of course, the first people I practice on is my existing crew. I don't tell them that they were basically experimental subjects in my quest for greatness. Believe it or not Ricky was an incredible dude and had already possessed such qualities. Ricky was phenomenal in all aspects, and we were most definitely on the same page. I guess me and Ricky knew and had seen things that most of the other kids didn't. Maybe because their parents hid the truth from them. Not to say our parents didn't attempt the same but, me and Ricky were born under unique circumstances by movers and shakers. As they say, "the Apple doesn't fall too far from the tree."

CHAPTER TWO
INFANCY STAGE OF MANIPULATION

The freight trains were a thief's playground. Back in the early 70's to mid-80s we had freight trains that came through our neighborhoods. The freights hauled cases of beer, furniture, clothes and all types of household products. Everything from toilet paper, cereal, to Newport cigarettes. Any and everything was on those freight trains. They even once came through with mini motorbikes. But nevertheless, I personally found out about the freight trains while one day standing in front of my Grandparents house. A guy named Selwyn and his crew came by carrying boxes of only God knows what. But he yelled. "Hey everybody the freight is back in town!" All the crooks went running around the corner in the direction of the freights. Me, Ricky and John followed just to be nosey, and we were amazed at what we witnessed. There were so many people from the neighborhood carrying boxes of Kool cigarettes. Mind you the train is parked during this time because a

Caboose drops off the train then another is to come later and take it to its destination.

Nevertheless, people would climb onto the train and throw the boxes off. They would take what they could and hide the rest in the bushes. Only to return later to steal more boxes and to return to their stolen stashes. It didn't take a genius to ascertain where my mind was at. Yes, I convinced Ricky and John to help me steal their stashes. Now I have a new plan. I tell Ricky and John that we need to go to the freight everyday just to see if it was back in town but, if it's back in town we should keep it to ourselves. The same night after we all went home for dinner, I told them to return to my Grandparent's basement so we could incorporate our newly found hustle into our organization. Yes, at ten or eleven years old we were young entrepreneurs. If it didn't make money, then it didn't make no sense. Nevertheless, we literally pull-out pen and paper and write down step by step how to enter the freight yard without people from the neighborhood seeing us. The plan was to walk to Ridgewood, which was an Italian area at the time. Climb a rock hill which was rather tall and steep, but we all took our chances. After reaching the top of the hill we would walk back to our neighborhood on the middle track. We did this every day for about a week before we saw our first freight train. Yeah, we jumped for joy hoping we struck hood gold. The way we entered the trains we would throw rocks at the train walls if it made a loud echo noise it meant the train was empty. If it made a thump, we knew the container was packed with goods. At least twenty trains were connected and after hitting about twelve we struck ghetto gold. I can't remember exactly what we stole off those trains that day, but we cleaned it out. I told Ricky and John to go back to the block while I unloaded the train and stash the boxes. They went to the block to get three shopping carts we had taken from Key Food weeks before anticipating this very moment. I also told them to bring three sheets out of my grandparent's backyard. Like I said, we had planned this heist to the T.

  Anyway, I'm working hard, lifting boxes and carrying them to the edge as I wait for my team to return and by the time Ricky and John arrive to the freight, the car is totally empty. Now all I had to do is slide them down the steep hill with ease and place the stolen goods in the shopping carts. We covered them with the sheets and trooped it back to Bushwick. When we get back, we sneak into my Grandparent's backyard, only to find them setting up for a cookout. My uncle Dee and Grandpa say, "hey what do you boys have there?" I say, "nothing Uncle Dee." My uncle Dee says, "Boogaloo what do you have there?" My Grandpa says, "ain't no telling what the hell them boys got in those carts!" Uncle Dee walks over to where we were and looked inside of the carts and says "where the hell did you get all of this damn dog food? From the looks of it, I know y'all did some illegal shit!" My Grandpa sneaks in the house to call my mom and Royce. When they show up, Mom slaps me upside the head and marched me to the basement. Boy, was she upset. "Ricky and John bring your ass in this basement too!" She yelled. Once downstairs Royce gets ready to chastise us and my mom says "Royce please! Boogaloo what did you boys do?' John tells her that we robbed the freight trains, and we have more boxes stashed. My mother looks at Royce, he shakes his head and throw my mother the keys to his dump truck. Off we went to the site to pick up the rest of the boxes. My mom was a mess! Come to think of it, my mom was tougher and meaner than half the men in the neighborhood. As I got older, I find out my mom put in some serious work in and around the neighborhood. In fact, I think it was one of the reasons Royce was attracted to her. They were on some Bonnie and Clyde shit. Boy, do I wish they could have stayed together. Moving right along, now we are in Royce's dump truck stopping at every corner store selling boxes of dog food. Man, we made a fortune! So now we have several hustles. Packing bags, squeegeeing, pumping gas and robbing freight trains! Later that week Royce sits me down and tells me he was upset with me because I was moving backwards. He said I should use my brain better. He asked me why was I putting myself in a bad situation?

He also said he admired ethic, but stealing was fucked up and plus tasteless! Man did I feel bad. I felt like I had disappointed my male superhero. So, I devised a plan. I told Ricky to get some kids together to have them help him do the freight jobs because I was working on a bigger scheme.

CHAPTER THREE
BUILD AND DESTROY

I joined the Bushwick Royal Cadets and stayed for maybe a year. I'm not too sure how long it was but inside the cadets I learned a lot about self-esteem and discipline which helped me in years to come. How did I manage to do something so extreme that I was stripped of my ranks? My rank was given to a kid from my neighborhood (Dondré Whitfield) who later begin acting and landed a role on the television sitcom "The Cosby Show." Now that did something to my self-esteem, and I ended up dropping out of the Cadet Corp. Now I'm back at player's central. Back on the block! Tubby would often come by my house with members of the Cadet Corp. telling me to come back, but I was too ashamed, and my ego was crushed. At that age I had no idea how sometime people will break you down, just to build you back up. He said it was called "build and destroy." He said, he was building me up in order to destroy my counterproductive-ness.

Now that I'm older I overstand exactly what he meant. But at that point in my life, I thought he was being totally evil, and I vehemently felt some strong feelings about being demoted. In a sense I felt vengeful and venomous toward Dondré because he received my ranks. So, I refused to go back. But nevertheless, I'm back on the block of Wilson Avenue. Right there in the mix of the belly of the beast. Right back at home.

CHAPTER FOUR
PEACE LITTLE GOD

Lord Sincere, I must admit the first time I met him he had about seven guys with him. I'm standing in front of Royce's record shop. Royce is standing by me, and we are both listening to Sincere. He's in a cypher teaching his students. I remember him quoting the eight degrees in the one forty. Which was what makes rain, hail, snow and earthquakes? Lord Sincere quotes this with lightning speed. I must admit I was mesmerized and totally impressed. He was so cool and swift; he had the attention of all the people in front of the record shop. There were some who would interrupt him and say shit like "if you are God then walk on air, or if you God then do this or do that." His response was "brother you're so dumb, deaf and blind that you still believe in a mystery God. It seemed as if every word he spoke, he would look over at me and wink his eye. Royce caught him and told me to go into the record shop. I assume he didn't want me to believe in what Sincere was saying, at least that's what I thought.

Anyway, I was fascinated by him, and I started questioning all the older guys about him. I discovered he was a member of the Five-Percent Nation. Come to find out he was one of the leaders of the Five Percenters. He had a crew of students and was followed by both male and female. Not only was he smart and fly, but he also had the crazy knuckle check. Everybody my age and the older teenage guys wanted to be like Sincere. He had all the girls, all the props and full of wisdom. During this time everybody in the neighborhood was either converting to Muslim or Five Percenter and I myself went with the flow. Black men all over the world was trying to find something in which to belong. By then we were sick and tired of the pie in the sky bullshit. Suffer now and get yours in heaven. Which was totally a thing of the past for brothers who were Five Percenters. It was easy for us to look, listen, observe and respect men such as Sincere. Especially once he told us we were all Kings and Queens, and that our history didn't begin with slavery. He said we were all fools if we believed different. So, every chance I got I went looking for Sincere. Come to find out he lived down the block from my house. I didn't know that in the beginning because he never hung around the way. He was always at this school for Gods and Earths up in Harlem. Nevertheless, I would walk down the block in hopes of seeing him and he paid me no attention. Then one day I'm standing on the corner talking to Roland and James. When I saw him, I said to them "Peace God I'm leaving!" Loud enough for Sincere to hear me. He then looked out of his window and laughed. Roland and James had no idea what I was even talking about when I shook their hands and said Peace God. I only did that to get the attention of Sincere and it worked. Roland later became Powerful Truth. My true road dog and partner in crime. Anyway, maybe a week or so later I'm back at player's central talking shit, swallowing spit and here comes Lord Sincere, Born Truth, Wise Allah, and Freedom. They formed a cypher and I run out of the record shop to get a front row view and wait for them to start building (enlightening). Sincere looks at me and says, "Peace little God." I said, "are you talking to me?"

He says, "yes little God. Weren't you with the young gods in front of my crib the other day? Didn't I hear you say peace Gods to those young Gods?" "Yes," I answered. He said what is your name. I say, "Boogaloo." He said, "damn little god what does that mean? First, in order to be God you have to get rid of the devil's name." I said, "the devil didn't give me my name, my mom did and don't be calling her no damn devil!" They all laughed. Lord Sincere said, "little God you're something else. I can clearly see you are hungry for knowledge of self. Either that, or you think it's cool. Which one?" I said, "I think it's cool.". He said yeah, it's cool to know your history, nothing more, nothing less. Royce comes outside and slaps Lord Sincere a five. He put his arm around him, and they walk around the corner. Royce comes back alone and Sincere goes the other way.

The very next day, after school. Sincere is standing on the corner of my school wearing a pair of shark shin pants, a mock neck shirt and a pair of British Walker shoes. My mother is standing next to him, and she introduces us. I say, "ma I know him. This is the nigga who said you gave me a devil's name." My mom laughed and said after you do your homework, I want you to go down to Angel's house. Angel was Sincere's mother. When I finished my homework, I rushed down to Angel's only to find Sincere teaching lessons. Almost all the kids in the neighborhood were in attendance. It was then Sincere explained to me how our history didn't start with us being slaves, and the trans-Atlantic trade. He explained to me how we were Kings and Queens and how the dissatisfied tricked us into slavery. He said something to the effects of how we were promised more gold for our labor in this new world. Before I met Sincere, I had no knowledge of our supreme existence. The more he taught, the more I desired to learn.

CHAPTER FIVE
UNIQUE IS BORN

Within sixty days I had already mastered the one twenty which were the lessons we were taught. After leaving one twenty, I became kind of rebellious in school. One day while in class, we were being taught about Christopher Columbus. The teacher was explaining how he discovered America. I interjected and asked the teacher how could Columbus discover America when the Indians were already there? And why was she teaching us that he was a great man when he was a thief, a murderer and not to leave out he was also rapist? And what's more frightening is, you are a woman of color! Is it because you were misinformed, indoctrinated or you just ain't got no love for young people, let alone yourself!"

Boy, did she get mad! She sent me straight to the dean's office for disrupting the class. Later that evening my mom got a call from my teacher about what I said in class. I went into the kitchen and picked up the phone so

I could listen to what she had to say. My mom asked her did I lie or was I merely asking questions which I was seeking answers for? She begins to tell my mom it was ironic how I opened her eyes. She said she never looked at it that way and said it was basic common sense, but we were so caught up in allowing these people to create a manuscript to how we should live our lives until we disregarded the obvious. She said Ms. Battle when your son stood up and asked "why are you teaching us, trick knowledge? I bet you eat on thanksgiving instead of fasting and praying for all those Indians. He asked if I knew that men, women and children were slaughtered. In closing, he said Damn you are lost!" She continued to explain to my mom how I challenged her power and control of the classroom.

"So now school it's about power and control huh? I interjected. Not about education? I asked. Before she could answer, I said. It's crazy how you are knowingly misinforming us! Mom she's a participant of the ten percenters. She knows the truth yet she's willing

to deceive her own kind for more food, and gold. She's a sellout and she's willing to sellout her very own!" My

Mom let me complete my statement and then yelled "boy get off the phone!" I pretended to hang up but instead I stayed on the line and listened. The teacher said "Ms. Battle he is an extremely unique kid, but I can't allow him to continue to disrupt the class. "So, what he's saying is a fact. Isn't it?" My Mom asked. "What are you speaking of?" She replied. "So, what you're telling me is because my son knows the truth, he should be punished?" My mom asked. Then hung up on the teacher! The very next day as I'm standing in the lineup yard I was approached by a few fellow classmates. They say, "Damn Boogaloo we didn't know you were so smart!" I say to them "all black men have the same power! Don't y'all know the Black man is God!" I was saying to them what Sincere said to me. "Man, we are bigger and wiser, and you will never know unless you get knowledge of self. Do y'all want knowledge of self?" I asked. "Yes!" They all say. "Well, when they ask us to stand up to pledge allegiance to their flag you will stay seated. And you Michael Riley throw away your ham sandwich!" (He did.) Once we reach the class, the speakers come on and the principal says, "Everyone please stand for the allegiance." We all stay seated, and the teacher says fellas please stand. I then stood up and spoke. "Are you seriously telling a group of people who were hung, murdered and raped to pay homage to the very same people who did this to us?" She ran out of the classroom. "Power is truth!" I yelled. Of course, I was taken to the Dean's office and this time Royce was called up to the school. He asked the Dean, did I lie? The Dean didn't respond. Royce said to him, "well when you're able to give me a correct answer I will speak to him about it but, until then I'll take him home for the day!"

Royce took me to the record shop. He said "boy you are something else, but you can't be doing that. Those crackers don't want you speaking the truth. You and your boys learn from this experience. Did you learn anything?" I said Yes. For one I understand a lot of adults are lost." "Yes, and the sad part is, it's common sense to what has transpired and what is still transpiring." He spoke. "It's amazing how they make school so important when they are only miseducating us." I said. Royce looked at me and said, "Boogaloo it's a process called indoctrination!" Royce explained that he was a former Black activist who was involved in the movement, but something transpired in his life, and he fell back. He told me Sincere was once one of his students and he was never going to tell me he intended for Sincere to snatch me up and teach me because he was serious about Islam. Royce then sat me down and explained to me that he had been locked up for a robbery back in the day. But his charge wasn't for self-profit, it was for the movement. He explained to me why it is important to not let your enemy know how you're thinking. I remember him saying, "the only thing them crackers gave us was freedom of speech so they can know what's on our minds. I understood.

CHAPTER SIX
POWER

At this point in my life, I start to see the educational system as a systematic plot to keep us enslaved and to keep us separated as a people. At a very early age I overstood we were not an inferior race. Shit, how can we be inferior when we were the first people on the planet, and we came from God! However, knowing this at an early age made me extremely rebellious as a youth. As a child I overstood messages which were given to me by the likes of Sincere. I overstood that he wanted to see us rise as a Black race and to bring us out of a mental state of slavery! It didn't take a genius to ascertain that most of our black leaders who we deemed as leaders had only endured because the government placed them in a position to lead, or should I say to mislead, and endure. Most of our black leaders, too many times have talked about cultural diversity.

However, those same people have been totally stripped of their culture, placing them in
a weakened position. So how could they have the ability to uplift their own race? Once I became wiser and more informed, I began to see the importance of Black Unity. So right away I began to form my own sector of the Five Percenter Nation. Me, Anthony, Michael, Darrin, Nathaniel and a few others set out to teach all the kids in our hood. Because I was more intelligent, I lead the group and we began to attend rallies in Harlem. We would ride the A train every last Sunday of the month in our best clothes and head uptown to meet with all the brothers from all over the states. By this time my mother was involved in my affiliation. She would knit me and my crew crowns with our Five Percenter names on them. Our crowns would always match our tailor-made suits. I must admit we use to look mighty fine and dandy. By doing this I started to over- stand the power of uniform. The tailor-made suits and crowns made us look organized and militant and we were extremely notable. We would stand on the corners building (enlightening one another) and people would stop in

amazement just to watch and listen. I would step out of the gathering which was called a (cipher) and lean up against a wall and just observe. I too was amazed at our brotherly love and unity!

Boom! Just like that an idea pops in my head. I say, "Gods enough building let's go to Halsey Park!" We walked to the park and start building again. I said to myself. Wow that's power! I then went home and begin to plot on how I could use this power for economical gain.

A few days later the school was having a candy sale. My opportunity had arrived, and I devised a plan to steal the candy sale money. I told Michael Riley and Nathaniel Brooks to meet me in the school yard during lunch, and they did. I told them that the school was using the Black man to sell candy that cost them twenty to thirty cents but wanted us to sell it in our community for one dollar and fifty cents and give us mere toys for our labor. I went on to make what I was saying coincide with our lessons, which were true. However, I had another agenda. Even though I have a knowledge of self, I still lusted for clothes and what we called the finer things in life. The next day Michael and

Nathaniel came to my grandparent's house where we went down into the basement to devise a plan. The plan was to go in every teacher's desk at lunchtime. There were five classes on each floor so, when the school lunch bell rang, we would line up and head to the lunchroom. We were always the last three on the line, so when the rest of the class went through the doors of the cafeteria, we fell back and ducked into the coat closet until the class disappeared into the cafeteria. I told Michael and Nathaniel to hit the first two classrooms and I would hit the other three. The money was in the teacher's desk in a box. I took all three boxes and dumped them in my school bag. We met back at the closet, and they gave me the money taken from the other classrooms. We ran downstairs and hid behind the staircase by the exit so I could take the money home and return through the side door. They waited there to let me back in and we went into the cafeteria as if nothing ever happened.

After school we all met at my house to divide the money. I told them not to spend their money yet, so we didn't seem suspicious. Well one bad apple in this case spoiled

the whole damn bunch! That got damn Nathaniel comes to school with a brand-new pair of
Pumas. When Nathaniel came walking into the school, I said to myself; look at this asshole. Michael looks at me and say, "this nigga is playing his self!" Anthony started laughing because he did the math. He laughed even louder and said, "Nathaniel you're mad stupid!" Up until then, no one had a clue to who robbed the candy sale money. Nathaniel jammed us all up!

(R.I.P) to my dude. I still love you boy!

CAN IT BE THAT IT WAS ALL SO SIMPLE THEN…. (WUTANG)

As you can see I occasionally drift from the story at hand. I do this because I try to give my readers a brief description of my life's transformation and to allow my readers to obtain the same feelings I experienced. I call them my growing pains. If for some reason my book falls into the hands of some inquisitive youth, they may be able to grow from the mistakes I made.

My whole purpose in doing so, is to show the importance of guidance and perception. The lack of guidance and perception is as symbolic to being deprived of the sense of seeing. Also, to show my readers that knowledge is not useful if you are not applying it correctly. It is evident that knowledge is power, and power can have a counter -productive affect when you're young, full of vigor, rebellious and there's no one the to reinforce your decisions. Because boys make mistakes and men make decisions. See the word man means adult male, human being and one must mature mentally before he can earn the title of a man. Some people are totally under the impression that a phallus (penis) determines whether you're a man or not, which is far from the truth. A phallus only determines one's gender. Once we grow into manhood, know right from wrong, and be totally conscious of the choices we make, we must take responsibility for our decisions. Again, boys make mistakes and men make decisions! So, in saying so let me continue my Saga! Having knowledge of self and being schooled about my history made me extremely rebellious, but at the same time the power was gratifying to the point where it was symbolic to an orgasm. The urge to (come) was more potent than the urge not to (come)! Power is just as compelling if not greater!

"Allah U Akbar!!!" Screams Sincere.
All the brothers run down the block to the park across the street from the god's kingdom. The gods were informed that Born Superior was walking down the street. Born Superior was none other than Rodney Bostick. Rodney Bostick was once a part of the Five Percenter Nation, but he only joined so he could get close to Sincere. But nevertheless, Rodney Bostick was accepted as one of the forces of security with the Five-Percenter Nation, yet he had his own agenda. Which was to rob the God's of their weapons, and he did! For months the Gods were lurking for Rodney. But they weren't really looking for Rodney. Rodney was a beast. Only one God was looking for him. No, I'm lying! Allah-Sun was also looking for him. Lord Sincere and Allah-Sun were beast as well. They had brought Rodney into the ranks, and he betrayed them and made them look bad in

the eyes of the older gods. So, a T.O.S (terminate on sight) was put out on Rodney! At all the rallies and gatherings this would be brought up. The (T.O.S) they would scream something to the effect of this "Born Superior is now Born Inferior!" If any of you gods see him T.O.S!" Months had gone by and the T.O.S was still in full effect. Me, my mother and Sincere are at White Castles. While my mom is ordering the food, Sincere jumps out of her car and runs toward another car. In the car it's Heavy, Carl, and the infamous Rodney. Sincere goes at Rodney and he backs out a gun. Heavy and Carl says nothing but, Rodney says a mouth full! (The beef was on!) The gods were well connected, so one of the older gods who migrated from state to state got in contact with different sectors of the Five Percenter Nation in different states. They sent in the trouble shooters from those states. They came and laid low during the day and crept out at night in search of Rodney Bostick. While all of this was taking place, I started seeing less and less of my teacher, and role model. He would drop by my house from time to time with a brother name Forever King and his brother Master Born. We would lift weights for a few hours as well as build. Sincere had brought me a weightlifting set and stressed the fact that body and mind complemented one another. Every time he came to my house, I would have a few younger gods and earths in my room studying. By now we had begun to incorporate science books into our studies and mathematics. The form of math in which we were so amazed with was called Sufism.

I took it upon myself to assume that the reason why I had seen less and less of Sincere was because he was on the lurk for Rodney Bostick (Born Inferior). But what I was later to find out that Sincere was ordered to leave the situation alone. He was ordered because Sincere was being considered for a football scholarship and the gods encouraged him to achieve his goals. See back then we were all big on productivity. Becoming rich so we could create a better life for those in which we loved. Lord Sincere would always say that he was sure a change would be made, he would sacrifice his life for freedom and for the betterment of his nation and he meant it. The God lived this! He dreamt this! He was this!

CHAPTER SEVEN
GRANDPARENT'S COOK-OUT

Marvin Gaye is playing loud and sweet. The DJ is none other than Tubby, the leader of the Bushwick Royal Cadets. He's playing this song because at every family event when my grandmother and Gina hears this song they jump up, singing and reaching for their husbands which would in a sense put all the attention on the men. My grandfather and Gina's husband sat there shooting the shit. Anyway, Tubby is playing Let's get it on, and my Grandmother and Gina are singing along with the song and grinding up on their half-baked husbands. Me and a few of my students are in the background eating hamburgers from the barbecue grills. Suddenly, we here (boom boom bang bang pop pop). We heard all types of gun shots! My Grandparents shout "those got damn diddy boppers!" And they continue to enjoy the night.

The next morning, we hear that there had been a major shootout in front of the Sugar Shack social club and the beef was with the Five Percenters. Word was that the gods had finally sighted Rodney Bostick and when they approached Rodney, he let off a few shots making the gods duck for cover. While they were ducking, he slid away unharmed. However, the owner of the Sugar Shack was a Latin man name (Papi) and he had a crew who were also gun slinging hustlers. Word was that he funded the community! So being that they lived such a lifestyle they were under the impression that a robbery was in progress and acted accordingly, but that wasn't the case. I couldn't tell you the theatrics that took place, but the end result was, a life was taken that night. The Five Percenters were now in a Beef with Papi as well. Word was that Papi came from a strong family. Nevertheless, the next morning Sincere's mother came down to my Grandparents to tell us the police were just at her house looking to question my role model and teacher. But even worst she held in her hand a letter she received in the mail moments after the detectives left. A college scholarship for Sincere to play football. No one has seen him since. The funny thing is that

Sincere had nothing to do with the ordeal because the guys who were involved were not (in house) shooters. They came from states away.

After Sincere disappeared, I kind of went into a state of depression and went back to boxing. But it didn't last because I didn't have anyone to push me. So, I drop out of Bed-Stuy Boxing Association. I start staying home more, just studying my lessons and history. All the younger Gods would come around me and ask why I wasn't attending rallies anymore. Then one day my mother tells me that I should go to see Sincere's mother because she wanted to talk to me. Once I arrived, she passed me the phone and on the other end of the line was Sincere. "Peace God." He said. "Peace." I responded.

"The word is that you are falling short of your responsibility." Sincere said. "What?" I replied. "God, you have a big responsibility! The duty of a civilized person is to teach the uncivilized. Just because I'm gone does not mean that you should fall victim! Love your lessons, not the messenger. The messenger is just the vehicle to carry Allah's message!"

He went on to tell me that my lessons were the key to upward mobility, and with that I will learn to love myself.

"Little God don't let me hear that you are falling victim to the devil's civilization!" Then he said, I have to go. Peace little God." Then he hung up.

I went home and thought about what Sincere said to me. As I was sitting on my bed, the bell rings. I paid it no attention until it rang again, and my mother went to answer. Then someone knocked on my room door.

When I opened the door, it's all the older gods standing there. They all say peace little god, what's your problem? The God is worried about you and remember we are a unit! You are great young brother! Sincere was flesh, bone and blood and the message is deeper than any man could ever be! Continue to grow little brother, we support you! Not for one minute you should think that we are not aware of how you have brought all those young gods to the realms of reality. Continue to do so! As a matter of fact, bring all your students to the God's Kingdom tomorrow after school. Then they all said Peace and exited my room. I had no idea I was being credited like this. This alone did something to my pride and ego as well as my self-esteem. But no Sincere, meant no guidance, nor perception. A monster was in the making.

(THE GOD SQUAD IS FORMED)
The following day after school, I arrived at the God's Kingdom with my students. But I had already formulated a different plan and plot. This was my way of showing the kids who looked up to me that I was a man of honor and respect, and I had the ability to dictate policy. Once at the God's Kingdom, the gods gave me praise and my students watched in amazement. This is exactly what I desired. To have the ability to organize and lead. (Manipulation is basic survival instincts!)
Man did I start to use the lessons for my personal gain. First, I needed to build a reputation. I already had a rep for a half ass, jive-ass fighter or at least a nigga with guts and heart. But now I wanted to be seen as a dictator, and a person who was loved and feared at the same time. See, even as a youth I understood that strength sometime comes in numbers. So, I would set up rally's outside of the neighborhood house parties, in school

yards, and on street corners. Anywhere people were gathered so I could have the stage, and viewers. This alone gave me visual power and the people were beginning to see the strength from our rally's. After I established a rep for having an army of followers, I begin to seek out enemies. Although at this point in my life I didn't really have enemies, so I created some. And the irony of the whole situation is that many years later I read a book written by Robert Green. (48 Laws of Power) and in this book it states, "if a person doesn't have enemies, one should create some." When I first read it, I laughed out in amazement. Because at an early age I was thinking like this and didn't even know it.

But nevertheless, I did create enemies. I would cause fights with older guys then scream (Allah U Akbar) and my students would go jump on whoever I created the problem with. That alone planted fear in a lot of cats. This is what I meant by strength comes in numbers. My team was feared. So, with fear being planted in the people in the neighborhood, I started to lay my buck-kid game down. I started pressing cats for their gold rings, chains, clothes, sneakers and would even go as far as degrading them in front of their female friends.

I was totally on an ego trip!

One day while at my grandparent's house, they were having a weekend gathering at the after-hours spot. My grandmother is serving a bottle of Vodka to a customer, and another had just walked in. My grandma says, "Boogaloo do me a favor and get Mister Ben a half of pint of vodka for me." The vodka was in the trunk in the front room. When I opened the trunk, in there were also three handguns. I took one of them and placed it in my waist, poured Mister Ben his vodka, kissed my grandmother and left.

The very next day in school (J.H.S 296) I start some shit in gym class with some guys who were part of a crew called the F.B.I (Female body inspectors) some corny ass cats. Anyway, maybe I was a bit jealous, come to think of it. I walk up to a kid named Red. Red was rapping to a female name Melanie and I walk by and bump him very hard. He turned around and yelled "yo watch where you're going!" I pulled out the gun and slapped him with it and ordered him to run. When he took off, I yelled "watch where you're going and don't knock nobody down running little bitch!" Melanie says, "that wasn't nice now, was it?" I slapped her on her butt and walked away. When I turned around, she was staring at me, and I said to myself "yeah every good girl wants a bad boy!" So, the next day at lunch time, I'm sitting at the lunch table and all the gods step to me and tell me that everybody is talking about how I slapped Red with a gun yesterday. I said, yeah and what? They say, we didn't know you were packing. I lift my shirt and say, well now you know! I had totally accomplished what I desired. Not only do I have the gods at my command, now it's on another level. I created a balance of both fear and love from my peers. Years later while serving time in Attica NY state prison I read a book called

(The Prince) written by Niccolò Machiavelli. In this very book it states that "fear lasts longer than love because people love at their convenience but fear at your command!" Besides, I was in this mindset naturally at an early age.

Again, guidance and perception are so important because had I had someone I could confide in, I may not have made so many damn mistakes as a youth. I was a fearless child. The streets and jail would later become my parents. I've learned through trial and error, and still I'm able to live with no regrets of why and how life had turned out for me. Needless to say, my bad decisions affected others.

See knowledge emerges from ignorance, and what I have endured with the blessings of God, I now commit my life to teaching. Whether directly or indirectly because I know exactly what made me fall short of being greater. As a husband, a father, and an overall human. Love is life, and life is living. Our youth are very special because they are our future!

So, the guy Red who I slapped with the gun wasn't really a tough guy. He was more of a pretty boy type who dressed in some of the finest gear. The clothes he wore was shit most hard rocks wore so I was under the impression he moved like me, and those who were putting in work. Come to find out he was related to Money from the sheep skin crew. Anyway, Red's little brother was down with them and at the tender age of thirteen, maybe fourteen he had put in some serious work. Maybe a week later a cat drives up on me in Halsey park and say, "what's up man?" I have no idea who he is. However, I say "what's up." He gets off his MB5 motor bike and says, "you are Unique right?" I say, "yeah what's up and who are you?" He backs out his gun and says, "I'm Red's brother and don't reach for your fucking gun, you are surrounded!" Little did I know my mother's side boyfriend Pep was related to two members of the crew named Danny and Tony.

They told Pep what happened, and he arranged for Red's brother to come see me while I was in the park. Once I realized I was surrounded, I noticed Pep was one of the guys from the crew. He walked up and told me and Red's brother to follow. Pep says "y'all little dudes need to hook up and get some money together. Both of you dudes are young fly ass cats. Plus, beef and money don't mix. So Unique this is Worm, and Worm, this is Unique."

Later in the week me and Worm hooked up. He had his team and I brought mines. We all met at his crib. We armed our soldiers and sent them to a neighborhood center where cats who were selling drugs, had basketball teams who competed for hundreds, maybe thousands of dollars. Our team would run up in the center and rob the ball players, the chicks, the drug dealers and the gamblers who were betting on the teams. This was Worm's idea. He was more experienced in the stickup game, yet he was younger than I. Me and Worm became close, but early in the game I peeped why they called him Worm. He was a snake! He later tried to set up one of my boys for a gold name plate chain and a nine-millimeter, but his man got popped!

So often as youth we flirt with death. Not that we have no idea we are doing so, we just don't care.

Hopelessness breeds despair and despair breeds death. In many cases, we didn't really care if we lived or died. Being hopeless and full of despair gave us the "fuck everything" attitude.

As time went on, I decided to stick with my own crew.

Me, Righteous Born, Understanding, Bigga and Nathaniel started our own thing. We became stick up kids mocking the likes of Derrick Worthy, big head Tiny and Baby Face the bank robber just to name a few. We came up with the idea of busting jewelry store windows. The crew would go to a shopping area, case out a jewelry store then make a move. One guy would throw a street metal garbage can through the window and others would grab the jewelry out of the window showcase, and we would all take off running and meet at one of our cribs. We began to make this a routine. We were wearing so much jewelry that others in our hood wanted to be down. We even attracted the likes of the Bushwick Avenue guys. Anyway, word gets back to the gods that Sincere's student is out of hand and that I was using the lessons by giving people knowledge of self, then using them to assist me in robberies and extortion. Doing everything the nation was against. They called a meeting. Me and my crew went to the meeting and at the meeting was Born life and Rakim as well. They were both called to come to the meeting because they were at war. After the older gods were done with them, they started questioning me about what they were hearing. Of course, I denied all allegations and went on my way. They no longer had the ability to tame or influence me anymore. I was now attracted to a different kind of power, and that power had nothing to do with being

God body. But everything to do with, "In God we Trust, the almighty dollar and the root of all evil." I was conducting myself like the very same people who were oppressing us. At least until I later learned that the only people who can be oppressed are those who allow themselves to be oppressed or who's oppressing themselves.

But nevertheless, I continued with my reckless behavior and of course, I was called in for another meeting. At this point I wanted to make a statement, so I brought along with me two of my comrades who both carried guns in their waist. When we reached the god's kingdom, which is what it was called back then. As soon we enter, Wise King Shamel went running his mouth about what me and my crew were doing and if we didn't stop, we were going to be dealt with. By then, I had enough. I looked at both my comrades without saying a word, our body language said it all, out came the guns. I then walked up to Wise King Shamel and slapped the dog shit out of him with the prettiest nickel plated thirty-eight ever. Just to let him know we were no longer under their banner, and we were playing hard ball. That was the end of my direct connect with The Five Percenters. I kept the name Unique, but that was the only thing I kept. I began to live like a savage in the pursuit of happiness. Cash! Cash ruled everything around me! Cream gets the money, dollar dollar bill y'all!

Big respect to the (Wu-Tang Clan) ...

(BOY WAS I MISEDUCATED AND MISLEAD)
Therefore, I try so hard to deliver a message to the youth today because like myself, a lot of them are lost and turned out. Only because they don't know any better and there's no one out there willing to put time and effort into the youth. A lot of the youth are too stiff necked and rebellious. Then, we as adults aren't giving the youth a reason to be perceptive. We must first lead by example and a lot of us adults lack the proper education, so they have so little to offer the youth. One of the things we must teach our youth is that peer pressure can be dealt with by obtaining strength and confidence. We must teach our children the importance of strength and confidence in themselves. I honestly believe schooling should start at home. Not by

an institution that was built and designed to enslave and indoctrinate. Honestly speaking, the school system doesn't teach our children how to be bosses but, instead teaches them how to be workers. In school I was taught how I was a slave, not that I came from a line of Kings and Queens!

The crazy part is, the obvious is so damn obvious. I mean never in the history of the world has knowledge been so damn widespread. At the same time people would assume that the dissemination of information would be free of bias and the product of real research. What's even more crazy is that even still today the schools are teaching bigoted half-truths, and historically inaccurate events of people, places and things. In no way should this shit be passed off as economics and should have no place in the realm of educating our children who will inherit a smaller and potentially more dangerous world. Seriously speaking, if this form of miseducation persists, we then have only ourselves to blame. Therefore, I'm trying to play my part as of now by constructing this never done before type of autobiography. I feel as though I have a duty to uplift my people at least! For the children, the babies! See half of the reason why I'm constructing this autobiography, is to reflect on my past, also so I can remain grounded. Isn't it said that "our past somehow determine our future?" See no matter of age, creed, gender or color one should always be willing to change negative energy to positive energy and push forward productively. Believe it or not, the one thing that is inevitable is change. And that's a fact! There's nothing more compelling than change, whether by force or naturally, one will change. I personally came to a point in my life where I had no other choice but to change. Like they say in so many programs, "to repeat the same mistake over and over again and to expect different results is pure insanity!"

During my stay here in prison, locked in SHU, (special housing unit), I began to over-stand my way of thinking was insane. I realized I needed to work on the way I perceived life. They say, "everything happens for a reason." I'm not saying in no way jail was my rest haven, but where else would I have been able to do some deep reflecting on myself? It's crazy how being in prison helped change my perspective about life. Here is where I came up with an analogy of how I see life, and how I should live as a man, a father, a husband, and a better person in general. This shit here is symbolic to death. A self-made tomb where reincarnation is mentally possible.

I thank God for placing me here, I know this sounds strange, but it is what it is. See it came a time when I had to take responsibility for the actions that brought me here. My negative mind-frame, my counterproductive behavior, people, places and things. So honestly this adversity was like me being reborn. It gave me a chance to put things back in perspective.

CHAPTER EIGHT
ALBEE SQUARE MALL

"Yo son!" Understanding says to me. I was downtown with those Bushwick Avenue cats, and we ended up in Albee Square Mall. I think it was up on the third floor. They have a game room up there with mad dudes and money getting chicks from all over Brooklyn. Brownsville, East New York, Redhook, Fort Greene but not one person from our hood. But the funny part of the whole situation is that niggas was talking about our crew. They had no idea I was the Understanding they were talking about." "What were they saying? I asked. "They were talking about all the jewelry spots we did and how our guns went off!" Understanding said.

He begins to tell me how he ran into a chick he met when he was in Spofford Juvenile Center. He said she was from Lafayette Gardens projects, and he was cool with her brother. LG was known for having the fly chicks who were boosters (shoplifters) and I wanted in.

The next day I wake up, take a shower, put on some Grey Flannel cologne, slipped on my silk shirt, my silk pants and a pair of Wallabee Clarks. I put on the olive-green suede joints and on each finger, I had on two rings. Back then that is how me and my boys did it. Thinking of it now, it was kind of extreme. But that's who we were and that's how we did it! It was a fashion statement! It also said that we were getting money, and at the same time it was a challenge to other stick-up kids. But nevertheless, after I put on my rings and threw on my YSL glasses, I head to Halsey Street to meet Understanding and Righteous. They were my road dogs. Anyway, Understanding had on a Fila suit with a pair of Fila's sneakers, and Righteous had on a Calvin Klein denim suit. Bottom line we were all fly! We jump on our motor bikes and head downtown. When we reached Albee Square Mall, Understanding's homegirl Red and her crew were outside. Red introduced herself to me and Righteous. Understanding says, "Son, she takes that money like we do." Red told us to hold on for a minute and went into the mall. When she returned, she had about seven other females with her. She introduced us, and one girl I was scoping name was Shaniqua. She was slim and was fly. I was impressed with her gear, not to mention she was a black slim May West. She had a unique personality. She was gentle, yet firm in character and I kind of dug that in her.

However, while I was shooting the breeze with her. I see this little loudmouth nigga come out of the mall with mad jewelry on. He had some other cats with them. "Y'all niggas are crazy! That's little boogaloo! Son ain't no bitch!" "Oh, shit what's up Kelvin? He said, "what's up Boogaloo? My dad told me you and the other lil Bushwick niggas be hanging out in him and uncle VL's game room." "Bushwick niggas? I say, you are a Bushwick nigga! Don't act like you don't know about that side of town!" We all laughed. He then asked if I'd seen his cousins Pop and Baby. I told him I don't see Pop too often, but I saw Baby and Jeff around the way yesterday.

Anyway, we stood there kicking it back and forth and then he said, "yo, these niggas on the third floor were talking about robbing y'all. In fact, me and my people ran down here to move on y'all. But when I saw it was you,

Righteous and Understanding, I was like oh shit, I know these lil niggas! Yo Righteous, I hear you are dealing with my people?" "yeah, a little something." Righteous responded. Righteous wasn't so much as talkative with niggas but, he had some shit for the females. Anyway, I asked Kelvin, "tell me something. Did these chicks try to set us up?" He said, nah we just overheard them talking about y'all and the way they were talking like y'all was some gangster movie stars. So, we came down hoping to catch some bitch ass niggas slipping." I said, "oh yeah, you already know what would have gone down out here!" He said, "yeah nigga pray to God I was here because niggas would have definitely tried to make a move. I say, "you know how this shit goes, dog eat dog world! The quicker you draw the longer you live!"

Anyway, we all vowed to hook up. Me and Shaniqua and Understanding and Red. Righteous didn't hook up with anybody because Kelvin was his girl's peoples. Oh, did I mention that Kelvin was none other than Kelvin Martin, the infamous Brooklyn stick up kid 50 cent! (RIP) What's so ironic is, in this game no matter how tough you are, or how tough you think you are. There is always someone lurking in alleys, corners, in the dark waiting to take what you have taken from someone else! It's a shame how we all lived in a circle. That lifestyle was pure sanity. Walking around with a chip on our shoulders, mad out of our minds. Basically, walking around with a death wish! When there is lack of sense of worth and perception is foreign, the final destination will be none other than death or jail if you're lucky.

The basic creed of the gangster, and what any other nigga in the game need to acknowledge is that; whatever a nigga in this game has obtained, if he's not shrewd and cunning, it is only his for as long as he can keep it. If he's not shrewd and cunning enough to build a defense mechanism that is ever so flawless, what are his odds? Keep in mind, the one who takes it away from him has only demonstrated the ability to outsmart his prey. If you're living the lifestyle, it comes with the game. And back then, you couldn't spell game without the (ME) I was the me in the game. Get it?? Man, once I got word the other stick-up kids were talking about me and my team, I went even harder. I went harder with fashion, jewelry, and guns. I wanted people to know, you either come hard or don't come at all! I wanted people to know that I was willing to die for my shit! I had a big ego, and my reputation was worth more than anything! Besides I was a small guy, and I had a short man complex. I felt I had a point to prove anyway so; I took no shit! Plus, I had over-stood the power of fear. I intended to play my fear factor. By all means.

"Yo Unique, this is my man killer B, and this is D." Fifty introduced us. "What's up?" I spoke. "Yo, you know Jay from the Fort?" D asked. "Yeah, I know him. Are you talking about little E uncle?" "Yeah, well he said, this dude Kash and them niggas was talking about running down on you because of some chick you fuck with from East NY high school, and you know them niggas run the east." "Well, you can let them niggas know I'm on whatever time and I'll smoke anybody!" I responded. Years later, I finally got to meet all those dudes. They were a bit older than me and when we met, they were impressed. Tut was this little dude making all this noise and I dug his style. He was smooth and at the same time cunning and shrewd. But his stance and persona said don't ever take me for granted! It was like 1989 to 1990,

I became cool with all those cats in C95 building on Riker Island. A lot of us got together and went gun to gun with some cats in the big yard. Yeah, for the record in the can (jail) they called me little Moet. We were all confined to different housing units for either knocking out cops or for being slashers. I was known as a slasher. Back then, none of us had any sense and we all lived like animals. James Baldwin, in his book, "The Price of the Ticket." "He is the monster created by the American republic, the present awful sum of generations of oppression; but to say that he is a monster is to fall into the trap of making him subhuman and he must, therefore, be made representative of a way of life which is real and human in precise ratio to the degree of which is seems to us monstrous and strange. - James Baldwin Again, knowledge emerges from ignorance, and boy were we ignorant. I want you to over-stand that this was the result of being stripped of our identity, our legacy, and had no idea of the natural conditions by which a human should live by. There are grown men who are searching for some form of identity and it's a shame but, as long as he's searching, there is hope! So, it's been said, "seek and it shall be found!" Yeah, we lived a rather abstract way of life only because we didn't know any better. No guidance, no perception, just reaching in the dark. Now I'm trying to shed what little light I've gained so that someone else can see.

See it's nothing for me to attribute my way of thinking to the inequalities that exist in the (United Snakes of Amerikkka). I can say that this country is racist, I can say a bunch of shit. It's easy for me to say I am a product of my environment. All of this can also be used to explain why I did the things I did. But a real man must man up at some point in his life and take full responsibility for his acts and his deeds. Before I ever came to jail, I was a slave of mental death and power. After you become aware of the truth and you know better morally, you can only blame yourself for any justice in which you receive. Remember justice is a reward or penalty for one's acts and deeds. The choice is yours. Whether you are rewarded or penalized is merely up to you.

But nevertheless, what I learned from this lifestyle and from my experiences, is the life I was living wasn't all peaches and cream. I was in love with a lifestyle who didn't give love in return and the irony about the whole situation was, I was lost and couldn't even see it! To the (Spanglers) - In Chapter Seven in the Autobiography of Malcolm X, he wrote, "Full-time hustlers never can relax to appraise what they are doing and where they are bound. As is the case in any jungle, the hustlers every waking hour is lived with both the practical and the subconscious knowledge that if he ever relaxes, if he ever slows down, the other hungry restless foxes, ferrets, wolves and vultures out there with him won't hesitate to make him their prey."- Malcolm X

Now that's real talk! Thirteen shots to my anatomy are a direct result is what I'm stating. "I became the prey.

CHAPTER NINE
WHAT THE BLOOD CLOT?

In the earlier 80's, in came the Spanglers. The Spanglers were a Jamaican crew infamous for murder and mayhem! Back then West Indians, and Jamaicans were making their bones getting mad money and putting in some serious work. Before I start to talk about the Spanglers, let me give props to Papa Gully, the godfather of Bushwick. Him and his nephew crazy ass, fly ass Vado! (Hines) My mother fuckin' nigga! Hines was so infamous that in movies like, "Belly" people spoke of the infamous Hines. When I say infamous, I mean infamous! I met Hines when I was working for some Jamaican dude name Ruly. Ruly was a dread whom I admired because he was a hell of a hustler. I was working at a weed spot in a Bushwick basement that was making like ten grand a day. One day Ruly left me at the spot to go re-up because the spot was running low, and it was a Friday night. Ruly knew the weekend was where he made good money.

Maybe an hour later some dude rings the bell. I look through the peephole and asked. "What do you want a tray or a nickel?" This guy doesn't answer. He laughs and says, "Ah who dis?" I'm like "nigga what you want?" He then says, "likkle motherfucka dis ere ines! Ruly na dere na mon?" I say, no!" He then says, "okay well give me a tousand dollas and tell Ruly dat Hines fi take it!" I say, "nigga get the fuck out of here!" He says, "you likkle pussy clot boy watch me gwan buss up ya ras clot face!" I say, "fuck you!" He leaves and when Ruly returns I tell him that some crazy ass dude named Hines came by and told me to give him a thousand dollars. I told him to step off!" Ruly goes bonkers and says, "blood clot Unique, bwoy you fuckin rude! You should have given it to him. Hines one bad mon!" Meanwhile, Ruly is shaking like a pair of dice, and I can't believe my eyes. Then Ruly says, "Unique you're fired!" Now I'm like, "what the fuck Ruly!" If this Hines character has Ruly shaking like this, I want to meet him, and I did. When we finally met, I thought he was a cool ass dude. I begged him to let me ride on a stick-up one time, but he never let me roll with him. But every time I'd see him, he would pull his car over and talk shit to me and say, "bwoy yu na ready fi dat!" He'd give me a few bucks and leave. He dug me. My nigga Hines.

Anyway, I went back to juxin' and robbing drug dealers, weed spots and number holes. Me and my crew started getting recognition for being feared and respected so, a lot of drug dealers concluded it might be in their best interest to put us down with them. Me and my nigga Righteous before we fell out, were tighter than a virgin's pussy. Nevertheless, for like a week my road dog is missing in action, and nobody has seen him. Not his brothers, his mom, not his girl and not even the other members of our crew. No one! Anyway, I start worrying about him. I walk down to his girl's house, my homegirl Chastity. She tells me she hasn't seen him either and she hope he's okay. I ask Chasity to walk with me down to the game room so I can pick up some money. As soon as me and Chas entered the game room, my boy Righteous is in there fly as a motherfucker. He's talking shit and flashing a mitt (lots of money). He had a big chain around his neck, a bracelet and two diamond rings. Son was shining like those diamonds on his fingers. I'm like, "nigga who the fuck you caught slipping?" He's like, "nigga I didn't jack nobody, I'm selling cocaine for the Spanglers and their paying three thousand a night." I say, "nigga plug me in!" "Yo Unique, if I plug you in, you can't rob these cats. I fuck with them heavy!" I say, "man I wouldn't rob your people." He says, "Unique, these dudes are serious about their business." I say, "okay I understand." Anyway, he disappears again for like two weeks but when he returns, he's in a blue BMW with this old Jamaican cat. Righteous calls me to the car and introduce me to Shock. Shock is a smooth ass Jamaican cat with Jeri curls in his hair with a big ass gold tooth in his mouth. He's like, "wah gwan?" I say ain't nothing. He tells me to take a ride with him and tells Righteous, "likkle more my yute." Which means that he will see him later.

Shock pulls off down Halsey Street and make a right on Bushwick Avenue. We drive down to the Muslim restaurant the Ansar owned and operated. Shock went inside an ordered two plates of food. Fried chicken, rice and peas, carrots and dessert. We sat there and ate while we kicked it. He tells me that everybody was talking about how organized me and my crew were and yet still ruthless. Come to find out Gully told him that he knew my step-pop, and my mom. He told him he's known me since I was about ten. Gully told him I was a hustler and a bad boy since I was a youth. He said, he knew me and Righteous were close and that he'd done his history. He said he wanted me to come along with my team and help build a spot with him and his team in the (Stuy) Bedford Stuyvesant. They had already had spots in Bushwick and spots in the stuy. But they were considering opening a spot-on Tompkins and Ellery which were the stomping grounds for the infamous gang called "the dirty ones." Shock had rented a store front from a man named Mister Lee. Mister Lee owned a big four-story building and sold three-dollar bags of coke which wasn't good coke. Actually, it was a mixture of coke, speed and milk sugar. Most of his customers were dope fiends who speed balled, which was a mixture of heroin and cocaine. The two narcotics together created an upper and downer effect at the same time. Mr. Lee was making good money from his three-dollar bags.

I remember the day me and Righteous opened the spot for the Spanglers. Me and some of the team took a cab to the new location. The spot was in between Tompkins and Marcy projects which was ironic because even back then, I didn't realize how location was so important to every business. In this case where there is poverty, despair and hopelessness; people try to escape even if it's only temporary. This is the reason for people getting high, in hopes to escape.

I didn't realize I was a businessman in the earlier stages of my adolescent years. As I said so many times in this book. How lack of guidance and perception can play a part in the decisions we make in life. Can you imagine if I was born in an environment where productive constructive information was available, I would have been on Forbes list as a youth.

In fact, most hustlers have the ability to create and prosper. But when information is limited and you aren't aware of anything outside of your training, your basic survival instinct tells you to be safe. Sometimes that's not even the case, sometimes one's ability to navigate outside of the norm just isn't possible. Because some of us have no idea things exist beyond our poverty-stricken communities. So again, we play it safe or even better, one is compelled to work with the tools we have access to.

Anyway, once we reached the spot it's set up like a candy store, but we ain't selling no candy. Once you enter, you get the vibe that something illegal is going down. So, I ask Righteous, "what's wrong with this picture?" He says, "what do you mean?" I say, are you serious man? This is set up like a fuckin' candy store which for one will attract the attention of kids. Do you know how much heat this shit will bring us? I'll be right back." I said. I went to the payphone to call Shock on the and told him to meet me at the Muslim restaurant. He said for me to call a cab and he would meet me there in a moment.

When I pull up at the Muslim restaurant, Shock was sitting at the counter waiting for me. I walked inside and we grab our plates and go sit at a booth in the back.

"Wah gwaan Unique?" "Shock man are you aware of what type of heat a candy store front will bring us?" Shock smiles and say "Gully tell mi say yu sharper than a blood clot! So, what type of front should we use?" He asked. "Design it like a number spot. This way it won't look crazy when people are coming in and out." I respond. Shock rears back in his seat.

"Come on Shock man, how many adults do you see buying penny candy and cookies?"

The very next day, Shock sent a contractor over there to rebuild the candy store front into a number's spot. After the contractor was done Shock pulls up with his crew. Him, Clayton, Face and Tony Tuff. They ring the bell and Righteous buzzes them in. I was in the back fuckin' around with Poppy, who was Mr. Lee's brother. Righteous calls me to the front. Aye "Unique! Shock is here!" I come stepping out from the back. When I reach, I see Shock brought with him a few rough looking cats who had guns in their waistbands. Tuff and Clayton were just watching me. "Wah gwaan?" Clayton says. "Ain't nothing!" I respond. "Tuff, nuff of the blood clot ice grill." Shock says.

Me and Righteous were fearless young cats anyway. The reason why Shock said what he said was because he knew that me and my crew didn't even fear God himself back then. Anyway, we all went to the back and sat at this round table. Clayton pulls out a bullshit twenty-eight grams and a pound of weed and throws us a pack of foil and some baggies. Shock sat next to me and Righteous and showed us how to bag twenties and dimes of fish scale cocaine. He told us to find customers by giving out samples. The funny thing was that even though we had the best product in the hood, it still took a skilled, seasoned hustler to establish this spot. For the first three or four days we may have sold five hundred in weed and maybe one thousand dollars in coke. However, Shock told us not to rush and to pace ourselves because everything requires time. Of course, that much is true, but the reality is that losers wait for opportunity and winners create opportunity. So, what I did was this. I went to a print shop on Tompkins and Flushing and had some cards printed out which read. "You think you tried the best, now check this coke and ses!" The cards also had the address of the spot printed on them. I started walking the neighborhood with at least ten bags of weed in my pocket. Hanging out in Marcy, Sumner, and Tompkins projects. Being I was once on gun time as a stick-up kid, I was careful to watch who I displayed my hand to. I mostly dealt with older females when it came to displaying my goods. In this case, I would show the older women the coke, give them a hit of it and then let them keep it. With the younger females, I would smoke a fat head joint with them, then leave. But before I go, I would pass them a card. It's amazing how the same skills used in the corporate world are the same networking skills the average street hustler use. The only difference is probably the product. This is why I said, "when information is limited, and you aren't aware of anything outside of your terrain; your basic survival instinct tells you to play it safe and again we only use the tools we have access to." Ain't no difference between a prostitute and a corporate executive because they both fuck people for money! Please in no way misinterpret what I am merely stating. I'm not writing this with complications or some form of many complex interrelated dialogues. In fact, this book is written in layman's terms so that one doesn't get caught up in the fancy or clever conversation. I know it seems like I keep interrupting my story with enlightening suggestions or what I consider food for thought. But let's get this understood. This is not an urban hood novel. This is a book about a real human being, and the purpose is to entertain. My main objective is to spark some type of energy or light in someone's head. I want my readers to understand that I don't think there's a child on this planet who is born bad. Every child is born innocent, however based on what the child is fed mentally, he can easily start to establish bad intentions. There is no one free of having bad intentions. Including Pastors, Judges, and schoolteachers. All of them at one time or another have had crazy or evil thoughts or even vindictiveness in them. Shit especially in the hood. Who didn't want to be a gangster? Not all, but it was common for a youth who didn't have a role model in his household, to want to be like a ruthless gangster, or a flashy dressing pimp or hustler. I give props to those who didn't get caught up in a false reality. When I was a knucklehead youth, I used to think whatever happened to me was destiny. But after so many mistakes and bad decisions I see different now. I know that whatever your mental state of mind is, whatever your mental paradigm is, that is what you're going to do. When you think crazy or negative, you can bet something negative will happen.

Back to the Spangler's... Within a week the spot was on and popping! Within weeks we were making like twenty grand between shifts. We had a P.M crew and an A.M crew. Me and Righteous were the managers and we basically just hung out around the hood promoting the spot and flirting with the girls in the neighborhood. But nevertheless, the spot flourished with ease I guess because we had top quality product. This work came to the Spanglers purer than a motherfucker! Like I said, the spot was flourishing like crazy and our job as managers were to build up a clientele and establish an honorable team. So, our position as managers were in full effect. Now our job was to provide each spot with work and collect the money so the odds of getting caught or arrested were slim. Shock really took a liking to me and Righteous and took us deeper into the organization. He sat us down and explained to us how the smaller you broke a joint (kilo) down, and the more cats who touch it, the more expensive it gets. For example, a kilo that starts out for seventeen thousand can easily end up going for twenty-four thousand. Depending on how many cat's hands it passes through. He also explained how the original buyer may buy it at seventeen thousand, and score like two maybe three points depending on his relationship with the buyer. But if he makes two points off it by selling it to another cat for nineteen thousand and that dude will then make a point and a half when he sells it for twenty thousand five hundred.

This dude will probably break the kilo down selling it at a hundred grams at a time, by the ounce, or even as low as by the gram. Somewhere in the range of twenty-four dollars per gram. At the end of the flip when it's all sold, he scores a three-and-a-half-point profit. By then, the kilo has no wholesale value left in it. But this wasn't the case with the Spangler's. These cats were getting a kilo for seven or eight thousand a pop and barely sold anything wholesale, so they had seen all their money. See with them, the kilo kept all its equity. The street level hustler is the lowest cat on the totem pole and may seem to have the pettiest position. The real deal is that he has the largest profit margin. By breaking the product down, he gives himself the opportunity to almost double his bread. A half of an ounce he pays three hundred and thirty-six dollars for, he can flip it and turn it into close to eight hundred dollars and so on. See the Spangler's paid either daily or weekly depending on your position in the organization.

Anyway, as I said before, we were business minded! We were trying to escape poverty and was serious about our business. After a while we didn't see Shock or his crew. We were given two sets of house keys to two different places where we would bring in chicks to bag the shit up for us then send them to the different spots to drop off the work.

But in comes the bullshit! The monkey wrench is definitely in the works. One day I'm laying up in the stash house with one of my chicks. Back then I had a couple pretty ladies, and I can't remember which young lady I was with. Shock pulls up with some cats. One name Deli from England and the other Lippy, was from a place in Jamaica called Spanish Town. Shock tells me to let these cats stay in the crib in the two other rooms and they are not to be left alone. He wanted me to check on the other spots to bring them along. I'm thinking, why would he have them around if he didn't trust them. I was entirely unaware that he wanted me to school them on how to move around the city. Also, how to manage the same spots me and my team built. See they were willing to work for less. But in any event Shock basically eased them cats into the organization and tried to ease us out. But how Shock did it, was by attempting to give us our own product and spot. That seemed like a cool situation, but we put in too much of our blood, sweat and tears to just let some cats take what we established. We pretended like we were with the program but, we were very upset and had our own agenda.

CHAPTER TEN
FRIEND TURN ENEMY

Fuck them niggas! They don't give a fuck about us so we shouldn't give a fuck about them. I had called a meeting at my crib. We came up with a plan to continue to manage the spots because basically our presence was very much needed in order to keep the surrounding stick-up kids in line. Like I said, we were a feared team and only a cat out of his rabbit ass mind would dare challenge us. So, it was in their best interest to keep us aboard.

Anyway, we came up with a plan to move Powerful Truth, Born Divine and Rashawn (RIP) to our new spot which was doing fairly good. Twice a week they were to do two days or two nights at the spots that were now controlled by Deli and Lippy. But on the days our team didn't work, I would send Derrick and Black in the spot, masked up and rob the spot. The Spangler's never had a clue to what was going on. But eventually they wanted me and Righteous to return to playing the

previous positions we once held. But we had vehemently felt different towards Shock and his crew. So eventually they did their thing, and I did my thing.
"Oh, shit son the word is that Deli and Lippy are fuckin' with Tabi and Mookie from Howard Avenue. You know them dudes up there be pimping all of them chicks." Righteous said. "Yeah, what happened?" I asked. "Well, they say, them niggas be pillow talking and word is that their spot fell off and they're plotting on the spots y'all running." "Oh word! Good looking for having your ears to the ground."

Immediately we devise a plan to have a cook-out and invite them to come. We spark up a conversation involving unity and solidarity and for them to allow us to utilize our crew when needed. They were content with that, and man did those cats get dealt with in the craziest way. Man, the stick-up game was in full effect. We would even send them workers who would run off with their packages and bring them back to me. I mean we did them niggas dirty!

One day we send them two workers, Freeze and his uncle Mackie. Powerful-Truth was to watch them, at least that's how it appeared. We gave Truth orders, 1. Introduce Freeze and Mackie to Lippy and Deli. 2. For a week or so, pretend as though he was playing manager. 3. Pay Freeze and Mackie, take the rest of the work and bring it to our establishment so we can have our workers get rid of it. Somehow Truth told this broad who was also dealing with one of the Spangler cats that he was affiliated with a crew who was running game on Deli and Lippy. He also told her Freeze and Mackie didn't run off with the drugs. In fact, they had no idea they were a part of the scam. Anyway, Deli and Lippy kidnapped Powerful Truth because they eventually ran into Mackie. Mackie explained that he was not aware of a scam. But nevertheless, they kidnapped Mackie and brought him and Truth to the stash house. Duct taped them to chairs and beat the blood out of them with pistols. I received a call from Shock for me to come over to the stash house. I had no idea Truth and Mackie were there tied up. When I reached the crib and rang the doorbell, Lippy and Tuff came to the door. As I walk inside, two machine guns are put in my face. Tuff reaches in my waist, take my 357 and march me upstairs. When I reach upstairs, I see Truth and

Mackie had been beaten bloody. I'm like damn! That's what I'm saying to myself. That day I realized Truth was a loyal, crazy tough dude. The reason they are beating Truth is because they want him to say that I ordered them to rob the drug spot. All Shock kept saying was "Make me know that the boy Unique was behind this blood clot shit!" Truth wouldn't say I was behind this for nothing. However, Mackie couldn't keep his mouth shut! Every time they asked Truth about me, he would offer them his phallus which made them hit him with more pistols and that shit hurt me bad. But we both were hopeless. Anyway, Righteous got word that we were in a situation and came to the stash house with our crew. But Righteous was smart enough to let them see he had the crew with him. That alone was a good idea because now they understood if worst came to worst, if me and Powerful Truth didn't come out, blazing saddles were in full effect. Anyway, we walked out of there and that was end of our relationship with the Spanglers. But the beginning of a new relationship with me and Powerful Truth. We became tougher than leather.

What's crazy about the whole situation and my past lifestyle is we sacrificed our lives for petty bullshit. It's crazy but when I look back on the way I lived my life, and the crazy shit in which I often did. I'm like damn Unique, God was in your corner. What strikes me the most about my selfish insane actions, is that I thought it was so significant and fly. It seems so futile and absurd to me now as a conscious adult. For example, the way I perceived success in all of it. Being known and being praised for ostensible reasons like stacking money or seducing women. Damn just willing to give my life for vanity. Although we no longer dealt with the Spanglers, our desire and hunger for the lavish life was more intense than before. Before the Spranglers, we were basically stick-up kids on serious gun time. Now we were seasoned, organized street PHD's who now overstood supply and demand.

CHAPTER ELEVEN
UNCLE BIG

Uncle Big comes home from Green Haven Prison. I still remember that day. Uncle Big wasn't my uncle by blood, however he knew my step pops, my uncle and my biological pops. He was rather close with my family. I guess back in the 60's and 70's, most men who lived a life of crime had no problem hitting banks and armored cars. Big had just come home for a bank robbery. Anyway, as soon as Big got off the train at Wilson Avenue on the L line, he came straight to my grandmother's house. What's ironic is, he didn't come there looking for my step-pops, my biological pops or my uncle. He came looking for me. Honestly speaking I had no idea who this man was. I wasn't home for most of the day, so when me, Righteous and Raheem pulled up on our motor bikes, my mother is outside talking to someone. She screams in excitement, "there they go!" Our reputation had made it all the way upstate to the max prisons. While serving his time, Big met a mobster who was connected to the boxing world but, this wasn't what he was involved with anymore. He was now involved in the smack (heroin) game. Somehow, he and Big became close and he told Big to put together a team and he would supply him with all the smack he needed. Anyway, Big snatched me and the crew up and we opened a spot in the Bushwick area. I had no knowledge of the dope game but, I had manager skills. I knew what organizational structure was about, so three the hard way was devised. Unique, Righteous and Raheem. Although we didn't see as much money as we did when we worked for the Spanglers. The Heroin game actually made more money than cocaine and crack. See the thing with dope was the customer depended on it because it isn't just a mental addiction like cocaine, heroin is physical as well. We learned that as long as you keep your smack at least an eight to a ten, you will maintain a steady flow of loyal customers. I still remember the first day we opened the spot, it was crazy! I couldn't believe my eyes. What I saw was what we called a cheese line back in the days. We had to hire extra workers just to keep the customers in order.

Powerful- truth would stand outside on the stoop with a baseball bat to keep the fiends in check. Truth enjoyed his position because for some reason, Truth wasn't getting any booty yet and he was mad at the world. Word was that Truth's dick was too damn big and none of the girls in the hood wanted to give him any sex. I thought the girls in the hood was just spreading rumors but one day I convinced a girl name Kiesha to give Truth a taste. Truth takes her in my bedroom and five minutes later I hear her scream out, "oh hell no! You are not sticking all of that dick in me!" Then I hear Truth say, "it just looks big. Me and Rashawn (RIP) are in the next room laughing our asses off. Truth had no idea we hooked him up with Keisha just to see if the rumor was true, and allegedly it was. Anyway, I guess this was why Truth was upset with the world.

CHAPTER TWELVE
PARTNERS IN CRIME

"Yo Unique, some cats from across the tracks came down here asking about this spot. I heard they work for some cat name Boy." This is what Truth is telling me.

"You said that to say what? I asked. "Word is that they came inquiring about who ran the spot because since we've been open, they've been losing money." "So, who is your source of information?" I asked Truth. "My cousin Skulls." "Who Skulls, the boxer?" I asked Truth. "Yeah, so what's our next move?" Truth asks. "Man, it's all good, we will cross that bridge when we reach it."

I walked into the building to grab some cash to make a drop because I didn't want the spot to have too much cash in it. I did this frequently just in case the police came to raid the spot. I get the money, go downstairs and call Raheem to come pick-up and make the drop. While waiting, I went inside one of the apartments on the first floor because I was sleeping around with a chic at least twenty years my senior. Her name was Deloris. Deloris had and still has the fattest ass I ever seen. I called her Duck whenever I saw her. I still remember the day I met Duck. I was wearing a brown silk shirt, some beige slacks and a pair of brown suede Bally shoes. Righteous had on a linen short suit and a pair of Bally shoes. Raheem had on a velour prince suit he copped from Ralphie's. Truth had on a pair of Clarks and some slacks. I remember the day like it was yesterday. Anyway, Deloris would always come on the stoop in front of the spot and flirt with me. I had no idea I had the ability to pull a grown ass woman.

Especially a woman as beautiful as Deloris. But nevertheless, in the beginning all my homeboys were like Unique the only reason she be on you is because you're making money. They were unaware she had never spoken of money in my presence. Let alone ask me for any! She later told me she was attracted to me, not so much for my physical appearance but, my lifestyle and compelling persona. Plus, she added that although I was always on my dictator shit, she knew my job description required that. And underneath all the armored shell of bravado she knew I was a compassionate dude. I asked her how did she know this? She explained to me that she observed how I catered to all the fatherless kids in the building whose fathers were absent due to either death, drugs or prison. The building we occupied was a drug haven so most of the kid's parents were addicted to drugs. She asked me how could I relate to those kids when Royce was my Dad, and my upbringing was much different than those fatherless children? I never told Deloris that Royce wasn't my biological pops and how I secretly longed for acceptance and love from my real father. So, when I saw other kids with a similar situation, I secretly felt their pain. As time progressed, me and Deloris became rather tight. My mother didn't approve of our relationship and somehow threw a monkey wrench in the works. She didn't approve of me dealing with an older woman which is ironic considering she was extremely attracted to younger men. Before Deloris and I ended our friendship, I introduced Truth to one of her homegirls who was twenty–thirty years his senior. I won't mention her name because to say her name would be assassinating my boy's character. So, because we were so tight and spent so much time together, I had to hear his bickering shit all day. I figured him getting some pussy would tame the savage beast in him.

Unaware of the fact that Deloris and her friend had plans for Truth. My homey's character changed dramatically. He became so blissful for at least a month. Every time you saw Truth, him and ole girl would be in the spot all hugged up and in love. Raheem came by my crib one day and say, "yo please tell your boy that the spot ain't no damn hotel and we are running a business!" Later I see Truth and tell him Raheem wasn't digging him bringing his girl in the spot. For one, it's not good for security and we don't need the people knowing the inside workings of our operation. Truth agreed to not bring the chick to the spot anymore. But I also knew he was too damn hardheaded to listen and too ignorant to understand. Plus, he made everything a challenge to his manhood. So, of course later that week I came to pick up the morning shift's money. But when I step in the building there is a line from the first floor to the second floor. I'm saying to myself, why in the hell are all these fiends in the hallway like this? For security purposes, I pull out my gun and tell everybody to back up because there could easily be a stick-up kid in the mix. Shit, this was a golden opportunity to catch a player slipping. I go up to see what's the hold up. In the mix of the crowd, I spot Truth's cousin Skull, so my guard went up instantly. Then I immediately remembered the conversation me and Truth had about our spot taking all the business from across the tracks. But anyway, come to find out this wasn't the reason why Skull was there. Skull was there because our dope was eighty percent pure. Plus, our bags were fatter so he would buy five hundred dollars in product from us, re-bag it and easily double his money.

Anyway, Skulls says, he's been ringing the bell to the spot for at least a half hour and there's been no answer. I pull out my keys and enter the apartment. When I walk in, Truth is in the middle of the kitchen, butt ass naked, drilling this woman from behind. I mean he's so into it he doesn't even hear me walk in. He's going off, saying all kinds of porno shit to her. I'm laughing to myself like man I can't even flip on this dude. He's finally getting laid. Then I set my eyes on the female and she's saying, "oh yeah Truth bust this pussy!" All the while she sticks her hand in the garbage bag and take out a rubber band of money. I'm like this stinking bitch is robbing this tender dick ass nigga. I fire two shots into the ceiling, which was stupid because a family lived right above the spot. But I was young, wild and all about the green. So now the porno show is over.

"Yo Truth you are bugging!" I scream. He pulls out the chick smiling. "Nigga you have a cheese line in the hallway attracting attention to our establishment and plus I told you to stop bringing these bitches in the fuckin' spot!" "Who are you calling a bitch? You short, big head motherfucker!" The broad yells. Truth thought it was funny until I bust her entire mouth with my 357 and turn her whole shit into a menstruating vagina. Now Truth knows I mean business. "Man, Unique, you didn't have to do that!" I pay him no attention. "Now go in this bitch bra Truth!" I say to him. "Why?" He asks.

"Nigga go in this bitch bra!" Truth goes in her bra and pull out two stacks. Each stack contained one thousand dollars.

"Nigga you are slipping!" Truth looked at the chick and say, "damn I thought you loved me!" I say to myself this nigga is insane, and he really needs a fucking hug. Me, Raheem and the crew call a meeting regarding Truth. The team wasn't happy with him and insist he must go! I tell the guys to give him another shot. I told them that I would be responsible for him, and they extended Truth's involvement with our team. Everything was back to running fine and dandy for at least a month. Then as usual, tender dick Truth was back on his bullshit. He let this same chick back up in the spot. Only this time she let some niggas in. She pretends to go to the bathroom and lets them in the back door. They come in and tie Truth up and take fifteen thousand dollars in cash and ten thousand in work from his stupid ass. Now either I deal with Truth accordingly or find these niggas and this bum ass chick. Thanks to this Spanish chick name Heidi I was dealing with in Brownsville. She told me her cousins had just robbed some lame ass nigga from my hood, and they came off sweet. She was unaware that the lame ass nigga was a part of my team. Anyway, I played it cool. For one, I wasn't concerned about the bread. I was more concerned about the act of treason on the female's behalf. Plus, I knew there was no way the damn money was going to be retrieved. The only thing you get from situations like this was an asshole full of time because broke, hungry niggas rather die before they return twenty- five to thirty thousand dollars.

I called up to the supplier's and explained what happened and they didn't go off too bad. They just told me that it was not going to be accepted again especially when my crew had such a hideous rep for being extremist when it came to violence and mayhem. I go back to the hood and tell Truth. "Listen Truth, this bitch violated you. She played you and definitely put your life on the line, not to mention mines as well! I told him that I was dealing with this broad in Brownsville name Heidi and she told me how everything went down. I mean everything! Down to how they stuck the gun between his ass cheeks while he was eating this broad's pussy. "You know chicks be lying Unique." He said. "Well, that's not the issue. The issue is the bitch shitted on our entire team and used you to accomplish it!" "Yo Unique I thought she really dug me, and I was really feeling her." "Truth, fuck all that love shit! The bitch dissed you and now she's telling people how niggas put a gun between your cheeks!" I kept bringing it up because I knew eventually Truth would realize that his gangster-hood was now in question. But in reality, no one knew about this situation but me, only because I was dealing with Heidi. I had Heidi sprung out on me and she would do anything to get on my good side. I met Heidi at Thomas Jefferson High School where my then girlfriend Cassy was attending. In fact, her and Cass were cool but, Heidi secretly dug me and I being the dog I was back then didn't keep it real and honest with Cass, and I slept with Heidi.

Anyway, Heidi would have done anything and everything to take me away from Cass, yet that wasn't happening. Heidi was cool to sleep with, funny and no hang ups when it came to sex, but Cassy was such a lady. She was intelligent and finer than snake eggs. Back then, I didn't deal with women who smoked trees and drank liquor. I was into women who displayed class. Anyway, I convinced Heidi to let me know where the chick who set up Truth lived. Once I found out where this chick was living and hiding out, I staked out this broad's place. I sent two females I knew, who were buck wild to hang around the broad's hood in the projects. I needed them to befriend her and smoke trees (marijuana) with her for about a week. I wanted her to get comfortable enough to leave the hood with them and she did. They invited her to a party on Eldert and Broadway and she obliged. But when she arrived there was no party. Only me and Truth sitting in a booth in the back of the hole in the wall club. Once she realized what was going on, she said.

"Unique I didn't set Truth up! Please believe me!"

"Sweetheart you don't have to explain anything to me. You didn't cross me, you crossed Truth." I stood up and turned to Truth and went downstairs. I walked over to

Allah king's restaurant on Halsey Street and ordered me a snack box which consisted of one chicken leg, one chicken wing, two rolls with, mash potatoes and gravy. I sat at one of the tables to eat. In fifteen minutes had passed and I head back to the club. Once I reach back upstairs this nigga is on some deranged shit. Some shit straight out of a movie. Truth was talking some godfather shit to this chick. I mean laying his demented version of Marlon Brando game down. I'm laughing my ass off on the other side of the door listening to his pathetic ass. Then suddenly, I hear the tables turn, she done flipped the script. This bitch joined Truth in the movie and turned into Pam Grier in Foxy Brown. Now she's being sexy. "Damn Truth, I must admit you do look sexy with a gun in your hand acting all emotional and shit. You're turning me on with this attitude. Why didn't you show me this side of you before?" I couldn't believe what I was hearing. I couldn't believe the extent this nigga was willing to go for love and acceptance. I smoothly step back into the room. "Truth, you are bugging! Move nigga!" I disarm Truth and once I walk towards the chick, the club owner walks in and says, there is a girl and two guys downstairs. They say they knew their sister is up here. Truth had allowed her to make a call. She called her sister to make her sister's boyfriend and his brother bring the cash back. Because if not, something real ugly could have happened. That was God telling me, Truth and the chick something because things could have gone crazy, but we never pay attention to the signs. I put up with Truth's shit for so long because I knew in my heart that he had true brotherly love for me. I knew I was only alive because Truth didn't give me up when those Spangler niggas had us at gunpoint and gave him a merciless beating in their stash house. All they wanted to know was if I'd set them up. The epitome of death before dishonor.

CHAPTER THIRTEEN
SHE LINED THAT NIGGA UP

"Yo Unique check it!" Truth said. "Check what Truth?" "Remember those Spangler niggas?" "Yeah, what about them lames?" "Well, I been fucking with the nigga Clayton's bitch for like three months now."

Truth explained to me that one day Clayton's girl was sitting on a bench in Halsey park crying. He said, he remembered her from when we used to hustle with the Spanglers. He said he asked her why she was crying, and she went on to tell him how Clayton takes her for granted and how he thinks he can show her love by showering her with gifts and money. She tells him none of that shit matters to her and she needs unconditional love. She also tells him Clayton had given her an STD and that was the final straw. Truth said at this time his spider senses kicked in and he went into player mode. Plus, he found this to be the golden opportunity to crush her fine Jamaican ass and Diane was one fine piece of tail. But nevertheless, our team was all about the dough. At least that's how it all starts off for Truth until he slips into slick Mr. Tender dick mode. Anyway, Truth convinced Clayton's wife to start supplying him with some good herb (marijuana) Back then the good weed was called lamb spread. Only a few cats in our hood had top-quality shit and if they were getting it, it was only coming from one source. Bushwick's Jamaican Godfather!

Within weeks my boy is stepping his game up and seemed to be taking business serious for once. I was proud of son but as usual, Truth forgot his purpose. He begins to believe that Diane is in love with him. "Truth you're a fucking Yankee! Those hardcore Jamaican chicks are not fucking with no American on some serious shit! I said. "Yo, Unique why are you so jealous?" Truth asked.

I couldn't believe what this nigga was saying. When in fact, I was only worried about him doing something stupid and them spangler niggas pushing his wig back. Clayton would kill his ass if he knew that Truth was indirectly pimping his bitch, making her break him off with weed in exchange for sex. To them, Truth was beneath them, and they couldn't have people in the hood talking about this type of shit. I tried to explain this to Truth, but he was not listening.

"Man, I'm not trying to hear none of what you have to say. Me and Diane are going to the movies tonight in Ridgewood. I want you to be there to check us out, then you tell me what you think!" "Okay cool." I told him. This was what I needed to see with my own eyes. Later that night I take a taxi to the Movies in Ridgewood and sit in the back row. I got there early because I wanted to be in the cut so Diane wouldn't recognize me. Once Truth and Diane arrived, I couldn't believe my eyes. They were like a happily married couple. I was like what the fuck! How did Truth pull this shit off? They were hugging like they were all in love.

The next day I see Truth and I had to be honest with him. Diane really seemed as if she was into him and was serious about their relationship. "I told you! Truth says. But check it, Diane wants me to move with her to Queen's Village. She said Clayton has a lot of money and drugs in the crib and she wants us to make a move."
"What? I asked. I needed to know if I heard Truth clear.

"I told you she's really feeling a nigga! He says. I couldn't believe Truth had this chick ready to line this nigga up. After getting the information from Truth, I immediately go to one of our partners Dae-Dae's house and tell him that I needed him to meet me at my mom's house. I explained to him that I didn't want us to be seen together in the hood. Because the shit that Truth had lined up, is going to be big talk in the neighborhood. In fact, we were going to have to pull a stunt like we got locked and couldn't make bail.

Later that evening we put our plan in action. I won't go too far into detail but, we called the cops on one of our spots so the people in the community would see us get arrested. When the cops arrived, they wouldn't find any weed in the spot because the 911 call was for trespassing and the apartment was in Heidi's name. Once we were arrested, Heidi came down to the precinct with her lease and we were released from custody. Like always, gangster Annie (my mother) came to pick us up from the precinct and brought us back to her house as we laid low, plotting our robbery. For weeks me, Truth and Dae bonded like three brothers from the same mother. We were close because we grew up together in the same neighborhood. Truth and I lived in the same building and Dae-Dae lived a few blocks away. I met Dae at a special school for rebellious kids. Day was a mess. I met him in the school's bathroom robbing three kids at shotgun point. Me, Truth and another kid from the neighborhood named Clint walked into the bathroom, Dae and this other kid name Plex had three guys laying on the floor, butt naked, and robbing them for their money and sneakers. I immediately dug Day because we were on the same page. Back then, the public school system in the hood was and still is to me is as symbolic to the department of correction. The same curricular exist. At least that is how I perceive it. Back then me, Truth and Dae and so many other youths, were totally lost and had no idea how long we would be alive. See as three fatherless boys we had no real idea as to how a man was to carry himself.

See I mentioned that Truth had both parents in his household. Truth's Pops was always busy working. His parents had to make a choice, to either teach or feed their kids and most parents chose to be providers, opposed to being educators. Most of the time it's because most of our parents lacked the education and/or the insight of teaching, and not to mention parenting skills. It was either provide or teach? Most of the time our parents were too busy trying to keep a roof over their children's heads and didn't have time to be pre-occupied with mental nourishment and building emotional stability in their children. Our parents perceived it this way because it's what they were taught. Unfortunately, cats like me, Truth, and Dae-Dae's perception of life were so fucking warped that the correct way seemed insane and virtuous thinking appeared distasteful and unappealing. The funny thing about growing up in the hood is, very few of us are of sound mind. How could one be of sound mind when murder and mayhem was an everyday occurrence, basically the norm. Hideous behavior suddenly becomes the norm for the Natives. See most of us who lived in the ghettos were brought up under a lifestyle that governs its own code and rules, which countered their own best interest. It's truly a shame how in the ghetto, an arrogant man is respected above the intellectual sophisticated man. Or any man with some form of moral conviction. It's fucked up that at an early age, we were taught to suppress our emotions and feelings. At an early age we were incorrectly taught that real men cannot afford to crack a smile amongst their peers too broadly, or often. Nor dare to possess a genuine likeness for another man because those behavior traits were considered un-mannish and soft. In hood terms, "a bitch ass nigga."

The person who displayed a hateful, vengeful, and vicious temperament, was the person who was respected, admired and notably recognized. But the reality is that you aren't respected at all. In fact, you're mostly feared and will only be respected by your equally miserable peers. Isn't that insane? How good men were despised, while vile men were praised.

It was the lifestyle in a ghetto of fatherless kids.

Subjected to and manipulated by fucked up values. I mean shitty, backwards values. Insane, hideous, deviant codes of counter-productive, non-progressive criminal philosophies. For us to live any other way was insane. Can you imagine the peer pressure one endures as a youth without a father figure? Believe me it was total hell. For not living such a repulsive life, a kid was totally mocked and labeled as a lame ass dude if he dares to think outside of the box and legitimize his life. I mean ridiculed is an understatement, if you dared to disclose a desire to be an honest man who desired to have a wife, kids and maintain some type of legit business to provide for his family.

Anyway, back to Truth lining them cats up! Word on the streets was that me, Truth and Dae were locked up and we couldn't make bail. We called Born Devine up and told him that we didn't think we were coming home for some time. The reason why we told Born Devine is because this dude couldn't keep his mouth shut for shit, and we wanted him to spread the word around the hood that we were in a jammed-up situation. Born Devine did just as we knew he would. Truth would meet Diane at my crib at least twice a week to go over the heist and use my damn bed to sex. I wasn't in total agreement with that shit and would complain. My mom would be like boy shut the fuck up, Truth is working his magic. That boy is getting ready to bring some serious cash in for fucking that chick! Still, I didn't like that fact that Truth was sexing in my damn bed. Besides, Truth was a sexual beast, I mean he should have been a got damn porn star. The shit that would come out of this dude mouth was crazy! Shit like "Oh yeah girl I know you feel this got damn leather snake! Oh yeah girl I got you reaching for shit that ain't there huh! Oh yeah girl call me big dick Dan." My mom thought that shit was so funny. Her and Dae would do stupid shit like knock on the door and say shit like, "big dick Dan can you keep it down in there. Then come downstairs and say Unique when we rob this joint you better make that nigga buy you a new bed because your room and bed going to smell funky! Dae-Dae was a funny dude! He was the joking type but when it came time to put in that street work, he didn't play. I mean this dude was on serious gun time. Back then there was only like five cats in my hood that had serious reps for taking money. I mean you had the older cats but our age not many.

Anyway, the day arrives, and Diane comes by my crib on Bedford Avenue to tell us that Clayton will be home around 8:30pm. Me, Dae and Truth stole a car and laid low in front of Diane's house. Within minutes Clayton pulls up and parks his car. Me and Dae-Dae slipped out of the front seat dressed like two chicks and walk behind Clayton and tell him not to turn around. He complies and we walk him into the building. I retrieved his keys but before doing so, I duct tape a skull cap around his head and face so that he couldn't see us. Once we were in his apartment, I buzzed Truth upstairs and I opened the door to let him in. Once Truth was in, I grabbed Diane and said, "bitch where does your husband keep that fucking money and work? She says, "I don't know what you're talking about! I then snatch her and duct tape her back-to-back in two chairs in their

kitchen. I then say again, "bitch where does your husband keep that fucking money?" She plays stupid again and pretend she doesn't know. Mind you, Diane already told us where to find everything, but to go straight to the stash would prove this robbery was not only a set-up but an inside job! So, we play her game because we can't afford to blow her cover. Dae walks over to Diane and slaps the living shit out of her.
Man, you should have seen the look on Truth's face. That nigga was tight, I was secretly laughing to myself. Dae-Dae looked at me smiling and I winked my eye at him and nodded my head directing him to slap her again. This time Dae-Dae slapped her even harder.
Boy you should have seen my boy Mr. tender dick
Truth shaking like a pair of dice. Man, that Dae is silly. He then tells her if she didn't tell us where that money is, I'm going to fuck you with this curling iron. Oh my God you should have seen this nigga Truth. Truth screams out! "Bitch where is the fucking money!?" Because now this nigga knows that Dae is in his crazy ass zone, and we all know this nigga is a jokester.

Dae rips Diane's bra off and expose her breast. Dae looks at Truth, and I am crying on the inside because now Truth is tight. I mean tighter than two dogs stuck. Dae-Dae then walks over to the kitchen and place the curling iron on the stove. Diane is in action screaming she doesn't know anything. Dae says, bitch now I'm going to ask you one more time and if you don't tell me where to find that bread, I'm going to burn them fucking titties. Diane screams and Clayton gives up and yells "Yo the money is in the mattress and that's all I have just don't kill us!" I rush to the room while Truth and Dae stands in the kitchen and hold them at gun point. I hit the mattress and load the two shopping bags up with the money and the drugs. Dae asks Clayton who did he want him to call so they can come and un-tape them? Clayton gives Dae the number and we head back to Bedford Ave with a big score. I mean it was a rather hefty score. We laid low for like three days in my crib. The agreement was to not to touch any of the money because we wanted Diane to be there when we divided the score. On maybe the third day, Diane came to my crib telling us that we were in the clear and that Clayton has no idea who the stick-up kids were. She informed us that he thought it was a rival Jamaican crew called the Shower Posse who set him up because there wasn't a Yankee alive smart enough or had the heart to fuck with him! "Never underestimate the next man's greed!" Isn't that what Frank said in Scarface? That nigga was insane! My team and I had more heart than most! See most cats in the hood were so busy competing until they're not wise enough to overstand that unity and strength gives you the advantage. Organizational structure was something that we applied. We incorporated that shit amongst each other at an earlier stage in our young lives. We had no problem booking or Juxin' (sticking up) anybody that was caught slipping as long as the heist was tenfold.

Anyway, Truth and Diane secretly kept dating. Diane then moved to Queens Village as planned. She bought a nice size house on one of the back streets. She would invite me by occasionally, but she didn't want Dae-Dae to know where she lived. She secretly feared

Dae-Dae's spontaneous behavior. Remembering that shit he pulled when we robbed Clayton was quite crazy. Although I knew Dae-Dae had a sick sense of humor that only a gangster type nigga would appreciate, he by no means intended to do any bodily harm to Diane, but he was convincing.

So, I understood why Diane didn't trust him. Anyway, life turned back to normal for me. I'm still on the streets caught up in the everyday hustle and bustle. Even though we came off rather sweet, I didn't take my share of the heist and invest it wisely. Other than trying to sell some crack or dope or weed, I spent most of my money on jewelry, clothes and partying. Meanwhile Truth and Diane are still an item and Dae-Dae was doing God knows what, but we vowed to meet every Friday night at my mom's crib and we kept our word in doing so.

CHAPTER FOURTEEN

SHE'S MISSING

"Who the fuck is that ringing my got damn doorbell at three in the mother fucking morning!" My mom yells from her room upstairs. I swear this better not be that got damn mi da microwave coming over here trying to fuck! And I heard y'all the other night when she told you no licking no sticking, and you slapped her. Boy let me tell you this, I better not hear that you done went down on her hot ass!" Ma why you think I slapped her? I don't do that nasty shit!" She laughs and says, "not yet at least! Now go answer the damn door!" My mom had a strange sense of humor. Once I opened the door, Truth is standing there with tears in his eyes. "Man, come inside!" I said. I then locked the door. I turned to Truth and say, "nigga what's your problem?" Truth fell in my arms and says, "man Diane is missing." I'm like nigga let me go, hugging me in the fucking bear hug. First of all, you smell like you've been drinking and what do you

mean that Diane is missing? Nigga go up to my room and sleep that drunk shit off!" He leaps at me and embrace me again. "Unique I'm serious!
Something is not right!" I then realize that it's not that he is drunk, this dude is in love. I became emotional, but not revealing my sentiments to Truth. I say to myself, damn this dude really loves this woman. I kind of became type envious of Truth because although I had been with a lot of women, I was still incapable of loving one. I guess I secretly longed to experience love, to give and receive. The sight of my mother coming down the stairs woke me out of that fantasy state of mind. My pimping instincts kicked right in, at least in front of my mom. I then said, "okay Mr. Tender dick it's too late to go searching for her. But first thing in the morning we will go out to Queens and check on your chick."

I'm sure Diane was somewhere in Bushwick hanging out with one of her friends by the name of Tarsha. Diane and Tarsha had been friends since back home in Jamaica. They once shared a rather tight bond. Come to find out that Diane was the illegitimate daughter of a known drug lord, and she was born out of wedlock. Diane's father was married and had no intentions of leaving his wife for Diane's mother. But this didn't prevent him from acknowledging his daughter and his responsibilities as a father. Diane was well taken care of, and she grew up rather high maintenance. On the other hand, Tarsha wasn't as fortunate as Diane. Tarsha grew up totally different. Tarsha had to rob, steal and whore for simple things such as Bun and Cheese and Water. Until one day while walking home from school, a team of girls ran by Tarsha tried to jump Diane. Tarsha intervened by telling her home girls that Diane was a ruff neck chicken. Because Tarsha had seen Diane at the Reggae Sun splash concert slice another female face for trying to rob her of her earrings. However, Tarsha home girls didn't acknowledge what Tarsha said and continued to run her mouth by calling Diane out telling her Go Suck Yuh Mumma, which is a very offensive phrase used to disrespect someone. Telling her to go suck her mother. Diane quickly attacked the girl, spitting a razor out of her mouth and cutting the girl in the face. I heard this story from both Tarsha and Diane.

I first heard it from Tarsha because her and I had a thing going on when she first arrived in America from Jamaica. Then later when I met Diane, she told me the same story. I would occasionally meet with Tarsha at Diane's just to do a little body bumping.

Anyway, when the morning came. Me, Truth and Dae-Dae drive out to Queens village. Upon reaching Diane's house, I begin to get this strange vibe.

Especially when I see what appeared to be the same BMW that Clayton's brother used to drive. Only instead of New York license plates, the car had New Jersey plates. I can remember every detail. Dae-Dae pulls up behind the car and I tell him to keep the car running while me and Truth go check to see what's going on with his chick. Dae-Dae says something like, "I hope ya'll niggas grips ain't on safety!" "Never that! You know my shit stay cocked and ready for war!" I said. Me and Truth make our way to the back of Diane's house. The house was strangely designed for security purposes. She had motion sensors in her driveway that lead to the backyard which was another entrance. In her backyard usually there were two pit bulls chained to the fence so if the sensors didn't alert her, then the dogs would. But for some reason her two dogs weren't on guard, which was ironic considering the lifestyle that Diane lived. Security is always an issue and a major factor. So, my spider senses kick in and I draw my gun and Truth follows suit. I'm like son something ain't right and to make matters worse Diane's door is half-way open and we can hear water running in the sink. I push the door open while standing to the side with my gun pointing inside the house on my mission impossible shit. Back then you couldn't tell me I wasn't a wild cowboy. But bet I wasn't stupid. I say to Truth. "Man, your bitch, your bullet!" Meaning nigga since you are so concerned about your chick, you have the honor of going in first to be her savior. At that point he slid in on the other side of the door while gripping his gun in a crouching motion and entered the house. I followed him into the kitchen.

Truth started yelling out. "Yo Diane are you home! Is everything okay?" I say to Truth, "damn be quiet! If someone is in here on some bullshit you are going to alert them!" As if being quiet at this point would do any good. We begin to start our search of the house. Diane's house was a one family house that had two floors and a remodeled basement that was constructed into a bar. The basement had two arcade games, a pool table and a juke box with a bar full of liquor.

I told Truth to search upstairs on the second floor. The second floor had two bedrooms and a bathroom with a full walk-in closet that held the highest of fashion, designer clothes and shoes. It was set up like a boutique straight off Fifth Avenue. I must admit Diane was a sharp dressing young lady, unlike most of the Jamaican women who tended to wear bright ass colors. Diane was different. Today you would compare Diane with the likes of Lisa Raye but maybe a shade darker in complexion. Yet, Diane was a fashion freak. While Truth was upstairs, I'm searching the downstairs on the first floor which consisted of the kitchen, living room, dining room and a small den. The den was set up as a small office. The first thing you notice when you walk in was a poster of Pam Grier that Diane had framed behind her desk. At the top of the frame, she had engraved on a gold plate. "Which pussy wan come test" Diane was the epitome of what they call today a "gangtress." Although I don't see any signs of Diane, I still sense something just isn't right about this whole atmosphere. Truth comes downstairs and says Diane's bedroom is ransacked and there is blood all over her white carpet. I point to the side door that leads to Diane's basement. I place my fingers on my lips and tell Truth to follow me. We creep down the stairs as if we were swat or something. At this point we both know that something has transpired. I say to myself, damn! I let Truth drag me into some bullshit. Then I snap out of that selfish state of mind and instantly remember him saving me on several occasions. I secretly smile to myself and say he deserves my loyalty.

As soon as my foot hit the steps, I hear something to the left of me. Before I can react, two shots ring out, one catching me straight through my side and the other tore through the back of my calf. Truth hits the floor and start dumping shots aimlessly in the dark, then I hear one more shot and then I hear a thump. Truth says, "Unique I'm hit!" Then the dark basement becomes illuminated because Clayton turns on the lights. Me and Truth lay there on the floor bleeding like slaughtered pigs. Truth only got hit once, but his hit was to the lungs, and he couldn't move a muscle. Clayton had Diane tied to a chair in the basement. He had been beating, raping and torturing her for days. Diane's face was battered and bloody with a piece of duct tape covering her mouth. Still Diane's face expression was cold as penitentiary steel. This was a special breed of woman. Even though Diane seemed helpless, she didn't show any signs of fear. At this point Diane was mumbling something behind her duct taped mouth. Clayton says, with an evil grin. "Wah gwan, yu have sumting ya wan say?" Diane shakes her head yes. Clayton removes the duct tape and says,

"Wah gwan sexy, eh?" Diane mumbles something in a whisper. Clayton says, "wah ya say sexy, me nah ere yu?" Diane whispers again, and Clayton walks closer and bend down in front of her. Diane musters up the strength to say, "Pussy hole go suck ya pussy clot mudda!" Diane spits in his face. Clayton raises his gun looking Diane in her eyes and say "ya wan ramp wit me?" Then boom boom! Two shots rip through Clayton's body. Clayton drops to the floor and (Mr. sick wit it) Dae-Dae is standing over Clayton laughing saying in a mimicking Jamaican accent, "Yu neva know Dae-Dae ere seen!" Then he moves in for the kill. Diane yells "Don't done him! Left his bumba clot ras right ere so him can die slow!"

I guess you know that he didn't die because then I would never incriminate myself in such a crime. Clayton was left there on the basement floor while Dae-Dae helped me, Truth and Diane to his car and drove us to the hospital. Years later we hear Clayton ended up getting deported back to Jamaica after getting indicted for being involved with a Jamaican ran posse. Word on the street is that some of Diane's people back home in Jamaica kidnapped Clayton and he was never seen again.

We later found out that Tarsha was running her mouth to Born Devine about the house Diane brought in Queens and that Truth was dating Diane. Tarsha didn't mean any harm in the matter. In fact, she was trying to get props for saying that she was dealing with a street legend type of cat. A true name brand nigga name. (Unique)!!!

CHAPTER FIFTEEN

TIME FOR A GEOGRAPHICAL CHANGE

After the situation in Queens, me Truth and Dae-Dae were watched with so much scrutiny. Because although Tarsha wasn't there at the house in Queens when the whole Clayton and Diane situation occurred, she pretty much had an idea of what transpired. So again, innocently Tarsha begins the same shit. Running her mouth about the shoot-out in Diane's basement. Like always, there are pros and cons with everything. Our reputation grew in both respect and fear. On one side of the game, it was fine to be feared, At least that is how I perceived it back then. But the reality was that the fear factor actually shut doors for us. Because giants in the game felt that we were a threat to their establishment. Because they considered themselves as prey, and me and my team as predators. Or we weren't approachable because most giants in the game usually are thinkers and calculated movers. Back then we deemed rational thinking for being coward shit.

Today I understand the thinking of hustling giants in the game. Jay Z couldn't have said it any better when he said, "If I shoot you, I'm brainless But, if you shoot me, you're famous. What's a nigga to do? When the streets are watching, blocks keep clocking. Waiting for you to break and make your first mistake." Now I understand that the people divided us because we were a threat to their establishment and quality of life.

But nevertheless, me and my team's names were being thrown around a bit much, so I started laying low in Bed Stuy. Not so much of laying low, I just felt like it was smart to relocate and make my bones elsewhere. Although my name was ringing bells all over Brooklyn, very few people could place a face with the names unless you were moving in the same circle. So now, Bed Stuy is my new playground. During this time, I'm living on Lafayette and Bedford up the street from Lafayette Garden Project. A housing development known for having some of the meanest hustlers, stickup kids, henchmen and boosters. I slowly began to bring my comrades from Bushwick to the Stuy with me. We would pursue the neighborhood in search of fly girls. That's what we use to call sexy females back then. We would walk the neighborhood flirting with women, smoking weed, and going to school yard parties which were called (jams). We called them jams because the school parks would be jammed packed with an array of people. I mean people from all over Brooklyn. Bushwick, Bed Stuy, Flatbush, East NY and Brownsville. A slew of people would travel from neighborhood to neighborhood in search of a jam. The school yard jams were equivalent to a disco or club. Both men and women pulled out their best outfits, cars and jewelry to attend. We were all like actors and the park was our stage. Hustlers looking for neighborhood stars and models. The women looking for men who were about their business. But everybody just came to have a good time partying, bullshitting and trying to escape the reality of the hood.

I remember on one occasion me, and Truth met some females at the park jam who were involved with two major hustlers out of the nineties in east Flatbush. These cats were getting money in abundance. But they didn't understand that most hustlers in the game have very few sentiments for anything other than wealth. Anyway, these two particular females came to the realization that becoming wifey or even being considered anything other than flesh was a situation where further progress was impossible. At least that's what I assumed because they started spilling the beans immediately about how much money these cats were getting and how easy it was to follow them from drug spot to drug spot and watch their everyday function.

I must admit these cats were most definitely slipping. I mean I witnessed some of the most outrageous slip ups a person in the game could possibly make but, these dudes would have made it easy to bring harm or even death to their wives, and family's doorsteps. But nevertheless, after weeks of staking out in front of their drug spots, or parking down the block from their wives or girlfriends house while watching them with binoculars, we pretty much got their routine down packed. However, we still didn't make our move because I knew there was something missing. I mean there had to be more to these cats that meets the eyes. I couldn't quite put my finger on it, so I chose to be a bit more technical with these dudes. By being more technical we learned that these cats weren't slipping at all. They had a plan of their own and that plan was to lure us into an ambush to eliminate us. Those two females that we met at that school yard jam was sent to entice and lure us into a trap!!! They say, "God protects fools and babies, and I truly believe that because damn if I wasn't a fool. There was an interesting phenomenon that operated in the Gangster and hustling world, at least back in the 80's. Crews and teams occasionally linked up or teamed up to achieve a common goal which usually was money and success! Unlike today anything that appears to project the slightest notion of strength we quickly eliminate. What happened was, one morning when me and my crew teamed up around four in the morning to start our daily surveillance, we witnessed this dude dressed as a bum lying next to my Buick. When I went to step over him a pistol went against my groin. He placed is finger on his lip with his other hand and said nigga, "don't you motherfucking move or I'm going to blow your ass away!' Truth steps out of the house and two guns are drawn on him. The man with the gun pointing on my dick is none other than Scarface. The other two gunmen were his soldiers. Damn we were ambushed this early in the motherfucking morning. We were unaware that mister Truth was up all night giving one of the damn girls a play by play run down of the events we had planned for the day and what time we would be leaving our cribs. What's ironic is that these two females had no idea where we laid our heads at night, at least that's what we thought. Come to find out the dudes we were following for the past few weeks were following us.

What's crazy is, that it shows how one can commit oneself. As I say so many times in this book, when one's knowledge and views are absolutely limited, the only tool that he is aware of are forms of criminal mind set. This is why education is so very important and I can't stress it enough. Why we as fathers have an obligation as community leaders to teach our children and expose them to different opinions. Because the energy that we put into becoming criminals are strenuous. I mean hours, way more time than a 9-5. I'm talking over-time and a half, not 24/seven but 25/eight. Imagine if we as fathers taught our children, both male and female how to direct their energy in a productive and conductive way. We must enforce this image of positive education and productive reinforcement to the extent as to where it is embodied in the bones, and to the souls of our children. Our children will then advance as human beings and become elite individuals in their community. Not to get off the subject but look how much energy me and my team put into negative behavior only because that's all we knew. I can honestly say without a doubt, that I have begun to attack all my negative behavior and images by stripping away the mask that I once wore.

Anyway, back to Scarface pointing his gun on my groin!! I'm stuck! My heart stopped beating and I braced myself for death. He stood up and waved his hand to a parked van. Four cats excited the van, searched and disarmed me and did the same to Truth. Then another car pulls up. I believe it was a Park Avenue Buick. Two individuals exit the car looking as serious as cancer. An older fellow exit from the back seat of the car and says, "which one of you is Unique?" Scarface says, "this little motherfucker right here!" Still pointing at me with his pistol. The older gentlemen started smirking and laughing in a sinister way. The way you see those people do in the movies. A movie like Marked for Death. Remember how the dread drug lord smirked at Steven Segal? Well, that's the same smirk that the older fellow gave me. I'm not going to lie I began to shake like a pair of Vegas dice. Like always, Truth is doing his usual talking shit again. I'm like this nigga has all balls and no brains. Truth is like, "nigga squeeze." I say, "yo Truth damn shut the fuck up! These niggas didn't come to kill us because if that was the case, they would have done us already!" Again, the older gentleman gave a smirk, but this time he winked at one of the gunmen who were holding Truth at gunpoint. The gunman slapped Truth upside his head with a 45 colt. Then the other pushed Truth into the vestibule of my mom's crib. The older gentlemen told Scarface to take his gun off me. Then he said to me, Unique take a walk with me. I complied and me and the older gentlemen took a stroll around the block. As we walked, he told me how he dug my style and my ability to organize and structure such a vicious outfit that was so calculated and precise. He then asked me where was I originally from, and who taught me how to be so shrewd? I told him that it was from watching niggas like him. He laughed then said to me, no for real where are you originally from? I tell him that I'm from Bushwick, down by Wilson Avenue. He then goes on to say that he has a very close friend down on that end. Then he asked me if I knew Royce? He's around my age. He asked. I froze!!! I couldn't move and became speechless. He then looked at me and stared for a moment then said, "I'll be got damn! Boogaloo?" I still was speechless. He stared at me again and suddenly a tear dropped from the older gentlemen's eye. He said, "where is Annie?"

Now I'm like who the fuck is this nigga, is what I'm saying to myself. This man knows my stepdad and my mother. And this nigga is beginning to drop tears which meant that this dude is somehow tied in with my family. Why would Royce and my mom know a nigga who's in the game to this extent. I had no idea Royce was a shrewd businessman and still had a lot of respect in the business/game in these streets. But what's even more crazy is the fact that the older gentlemen turned out to be Danny Lawless, the guy who used to live and owned a few businesses in Bushwick. He was sort of a family member because my cousin Connie had a baby girl by him. Now I understand why he had tears in his eyes because shit could had gotten very ugly. He could have done some harm to someone who he watched grow up and was basically family. When me and Danny returned from our stroll around the block, my mother is standing on the stoop. Me and Danny are walking up the block and I noticed my mother speaking and smiling with the two other guys, but Truth is no longer there. What happened was, when the two gunmen pushed Truth in the hallway, he fell into the door making a hard thump up against the door. Let's not forget that he's running his mouth which woke my mother out of her sleep. She got out of her bed and grabbed her old ass 38 revolver and peeped out the peep hole in the door to her bedroom that gave her a view to the vestibule that separated the streets and the living quarters. What she had seen was Truth being held at gun point by Danny's two stepsons, whose names are unimportant. She then yelled the two gunmen names from the other side of the door. From what I understand is that she didn't yell their government names, she yelled their nicknames that her and Royce had given them when they were just little boys.

Again, from what I understand she said something to the effect of, "what are y'all boys doing in my dam hallway with guns on Truth? That's Clarence's damn son!" Which was Truth's father's name. Then she opened the door and asked, what's going on? The two gunmen were shocked to see my mom embraced my mom and kissed her. She asks Truth what was going on? He started running his mouth again and my mom told him to shut the fuck up and to go inside. Then her and Danny's two sons went outside to wait on the stoop. Me and Danny noticed my mom and his two sons shaking their heads in amazement. Danny throws his arm around my neck and said to my mom, "small world huh?" My mom laughed and said, "nigga come inside. What in the hell did this little nigga and Truth do now?"

We all went inside of the house and went downstairs to the kitchen where we all sat while my mom prepared bacon, eggs and toast for us. As I explain the whole situation to what went down. God is good because if the two hench-men hadn't switch positions with Danny's sons in the Vestibule hallway, no telling what may had transpired. Again, they say God protects fools and babies because I'm more than sure that those two cats would have plugged Truth's stupid ass up with some slugs if things would have gone left. But like I said they didn't come to smoke me nor Truth. In fact, they came to create and establish some form of union between each crew. The reason they switched positions because the other two gunmen got paid to squeeze which probably meant that they weren't too big on thinking. Danny's sons knew that their tolerance was limited for ignorance or in this case a big mouth motherfucker like Truth. Anyway, an alliance was eventually established. Mo money, mo money, mo money! The alliance was formed, and our position was more security than anything. What I was paid for was to create a secret urban military group that ran Danny's day to day functions for his organization. I had to turn a bunch of hard head niggas from the ghetto into devoted militants. Boy did I have a hell of a task. But nevertheless, I wasn't going to let Danny down. Since I was old enough to remember, men like Royce and Danny were a definite representation of what a man of power was and damn if I didn't want to obtain that power. One of the most important skills I've learned while under the tutorage of Danny, was the importance of networking. I mean this man had some extensive networks of contacts throughout New York City and other states, which allowed him to recruit in many states and damn if he didn't. What Danny did with me, and my crew was unique because I noticed that rarely would he let two of his crews unify. But I guess in a sense our unification was necessary because both teams complemented each other. We also kept each other on each other's toes. Comparing how things were back then, to the way things are now, I would say that we were as close to perfection as perfection could possibly be. Loyalty, honor, respect! We conducted ourselves as men of honor amongst each other but, we were rather brutal and barbaric to others if I should say so.

Danny had given me such books as Min Kamp, The Prince, The Art of War just to name a few and those books took me further into seeking power. I was amazed with the stories I read in "The Prince" by Niccolò Machiavelli. How it's better to be feared than it is to be loved. because people love at their own convenience. I mean these books set off a flurry of emotions and reactions. Not to mention an unavoidably racial and political component that made me view life totally different in all aspects. Remember I had already deemed myself as a disciplined person or rather militant dude who was infracted with militant and anti-government ideologies. Now after reading those books, I tentatively embraced this new approach to living my life, and how to succeed in life. I became incredibly manipulative and eager to create a violent coordinating committee who were willing to do any and everything to become successful by street standards in this society of great turmoil and together we did just that.

Moving chaotically with no regards for anything other than money, power and respect! What's amazing is that people constantly forget that one of the greatest addictions in this world is power! We go to all levels to achieve the euphoric feeling that only power can give us and I myself was no different. In fact, I became totally obsessed with power and power only! When I first became totally obsessed with the street life, I was motivated by money. Not really understanding that the purpose of money was to make more money. I just desired to stack money in abundance to obtain all the vital tools that were required to live and maintain a certain quality of life. But as soon as I became in touch with power, and tasted the sweet nectar that power produced, money no longer took precedence in my life. I mean, money was still important only because it was still required to survive as far as food, clothing and shelter was concerned. But I was on a new drug called POWER and I chased it every day like a dope fiend chases heroin or a crack addict chases crack!

"Nigga answer the damn phone! It's probably one of those hot ass girls!" My mother yells from the bathroom. I go into the kitchen and answer the phone. "Who is this?" I asked. The voice on the other end says, "Boogaloo who do you think it is?" It's Danny and he informs me that I should meet him downtown Brooklyn at Juniors Restaurant at eight, and to wear something presentable. I agreed and hung up. I received the call from Danny around twelve in the afternoon, which gave me plenty of time to go shopping and find something presentable to wear for the meeting. I sat down at the kitchen table waiting for my mom to get out of the shower because I was still a momma's boy. When she walked into the kitchen, I asked her to make me some breakfast. She slapped me upside my head and said, "boy what's wrong with your damn hands. I'm your momma, not your damn woman!" Then she went into the cabinet and refrigerator and grabbed the ingredients. She made me a breakfast only my momma could make, scrambled eggs and cheese with bacon. A side of grits seasoned with salt, pepper and butter. Two slices of toast with butter evenly spread across the bread. The jelly recklessly slapped on the toast, with a tall glass of orange juice. Just how she knew I liked it. Then she made herself a plate, sat down beside me and smiled.

I nodded my head to her and returned a smile. We sat, ate and enjoyed a moment of silence. However, all awhile she's staring at me the way a mother does when she loves her boy/son. I can tell my mother feared for the way I lived my life and she kind of felt somewhat responsible for the path that I had chosen. But I take full responsibility for the decisions that I made in my life. Both good and bad!

After I finished my breakfast, I get dressed and go up to my mother's room. I give her a hug and kiss and tell her where I left money, just in case she needed a couple of dollars. She didn't respond, she just walked me to the door and stepped outside and watched as I climbed on my dirt bike. It wasn't mine, I used to borrow it from a close friend of mine name Hike. But nevertheless, I climb on the bike and start the motor. My mom screams over the motor, "boy be careful!" I nod my head, gesturing okay and rip down Lafayette street toward Bushwick. I was going shopping at a store called Ralphie's (SNA) which was located on Broadway and Halsey street. SNA had some of the most stylish gear that hustlers wore. Benetton, Polo, Bill Blass, Todd One suits, Pierre Cardin, Bally and Wallabee shoes. A variety of leather jackets and velour suits. Now remember this was the eighties, and SNA was a Hustler's Paradise.

On my way to SNA, I stop at a reefer spot on Reid Avenue where they have some good ass Thai-stick weed. What's funny is that when I pulled up to the weed spot, which was on Dekalb and Reid, I immediately get a funny vibe. The shit just didn't look or feel right. I felt all kind of tension in the air. It was so thick you could cut it with a knife. Once I pulled up, I noticed that the block was covered with an array of new faces. What was Ironic was, the soldiers who normally stood out front to protect the spot were now replaced with new soldiers on guard. When I drove up to the front door and parked my bike, I heard someone call my name. It was Hines sitting in a money green Cadillac laughing. "Got ya!" He said. In other words, Unique you're slipping. I started laughing then he said in a Jamaican accent, why you

a laugh ain't nutin funny. Yuh wan las in dem street betta ride cock and ready!" I began to walk over to his car and as soon as I went in that direction, I noticed that the soldiers responded. The team who I thought were there to secure the weed spot, were there to protect Hines as well. I now realize that the spot was under new management. Hines waved his hand and told them to stand still. When I walked up on the car, he had a 45 colt on his lap and an extra clip next to him in the passenger seat. I can't front the nigga was absolutely a phenomenal gangster who premeditated his every move. Not to say that he was invincible, but it was rare for you catch niggas like Hines slipping. That nigga was calculating, precise, shrewd and vicious. Nevertheless, I say "yo Hines mi beg you a draw." Which meant nigga let me get some free weed. He started laughing and said, "I shoulda let yuh a go up-stairs and buy some fuckin' weed. If I woulda neva called your name, you wouldn't be asking me for weed, you woulda buy some!" We both started laughing then he said, "go upstairs and tell Betley that I said to give you five dime bags." And then he started laughing again because he knew that I didn't care for Betley. In fact, nobody cared for Betley. Betley was a blue-black Jamaican with a hard ass accent that intimidated most, and he didn't really care for American dudes. Especially, if he knew that Hines dug you. I thought he was rather over-protective with Hines. So, I look back at Hines and laughed. He said, "gwan now bwoy. Gwan see Betley!" I'm like this nigga Betley is a pain in the ass. As soon as I started climbing the stairs a jet-black face peeps over the banister and started yelling down the stairs at me saying, "you likkle pussy wha yu want?" I yelled back up at him, "move your blood clot, Hines said for you to give me five dimes of Thai. As a matter of fact, throw it down to me!" I yelled. He was like no you must come up and get it. At this point I already know what he wanted to do. He wants to play fight. I'm like,

"Bet I am not in the mood for your shit today!" He says, "nah man I'm not going to play, just come up." I start walking up the stairs and as soon as I reach the top of the stairs this black bastard grabs my arm, pull me into him and head butts me. Then spins me around and give me a kick straight up my ass then pulls out five bags and throws them down the stairs and started laughing. At this point I really want to pull out my gun and put two in that asshole's head. But Hines wouldn't have allowed that so, I went back down the stairs, picked up my five bags and turned around and yelled up the stairs to Betley. "Yuh pussy bwoy go suk yuh madda!" That big black, blue motherfucker started yelling all type of Jamaican fuck words at me. All I remembered was him saying, "next time watch me go broke up your pussy clot!" When I reached the front door to the street, Hine's was in his car laughing. He like, "yuh a see ya bwoy Betley upstairs (huh)? I'm like yeah, "one day I'm going to smoke his ass!" Hine's laughs and says, "Unique you na ready fi dat! Betley one killer! My bwoy dat! Yuh no se the yad gyal named Tarsha that you fuck wit is

Betleys's likkle sista dat! Him nah like dat shit!"

"What, I don't even fuck with her crazy ass no more! But whatever, I'm out!" I slap Hines a five and told him thanks for the weed and jumped back on my bike and rode off. All awhile cursing to myself how bad I want to shoot that black bastard for kicking me up my ass. I swear if that wasn't Hines's soldier, I would've plugged his ass up with a bunch of shots. My thoughts drift back to Hines while riding down Broadway heading for SNA clothing store. I couldn't get it out my mind how this nigga always found a way to lean on them damn Jamaican boys. In fact, it really didn't matter who the fuck you were. If you were getting major money, you might just get an unexpected visit from Hine's and his team. Like I said I was infatuated and driven by such a lifestyle I really admired him. I mean everything about him was a smooth GQ type of vicious dude a straight pretty boy yet deadly. Kind of what I was striving to be. A notorious yet notable shrewd ass, smooth ass gangster!

Anyway, I finally reached SNA shoe and clothing store which divides Bed-Stuy from Bushwick. Meaning that it's sort of the border line of Bushwick and Bed-Stuy which were rivals for whatever reason. I won't say the whole Bed-Stuy but, them Howard Ave niggas didn't really care for us Bushwick dudes especially us Wilson avenue niggas. Anyway, when I pulled up in front of SNA you had a stew of Bed-Stuy niggas out there. You had Dray and Ali bob and his crew which was called Ali bob and the Forty Thieves. They had a reputation for boosting and petty stickups. I had already heard about and seen them on a few occasions beat up and rob people, so I knew to be on guard. Ali bob knew exactly who I was because he had seen me a few times at the school yard jams with Hike who was a friend of mine and his. So, he pretty much knew that I was on gun time. Seriously on gun time! Why else would I be a comrade of the infamous Hike. Anyway, Dray calls Ali to the side and whispers something in his ear. Ali says out loud nigga you're bugging, I'm out! That right there put me on point I Just started laughing! I'm like I will turn this nigga into a number two fucking pencil and fill him with lead. I walk pass his stupid ass and go inside SNA and start shopping. Meanwhile looking through the glass door at this Clay dude. This nigga is peeping inside the store from outside. I'm literally laughing to myself, because in my heart I knew this dude isn't in my league when it comes to slanging that steal, my gun. All the while I'm still looking for what I thought was a ravishing outfit. Finally, I decide what I was going to wear. I bought a Red Sergio Tacchini velour sweat suit, a pair of red suede Bally's and a pair of YSL glasses. I paid the owner of the store for his merchandise but, before exiting his store I went into the fitting room and positioned my gun which was a 44 bulldog. I placed the gun in my right hand and picked up my clothing bag so that it was concealed. I put my hand through the loops of the paper shopping bag so that the hand in which I held the gun was down in the clothing bag unseen. After doing this, I walked out of SNA to my bike. Like I had already anticipated, here comes this stupid mother fucker Dray. He was with Sha and Jah who were twin brothers. We all later became extremely tight, including Dray crazy ass. I didn't pull my gun out I just squeeze through the bag. The twins got out of the way but, Dray was more of a gunner. He slides in the doorway of the vegetable stand and started firing back, ducking behind a bunch of fruits and vegetables. Now I'm sniping hitting watermelons, oranges and cabbages and shit. All the while I'm peeping at this nigga Dray and he's throwing bullets unprofessionally and recklessly.

He had a form of shooting style which made it look cool, but the funny thing was that he was smiling. Kind of like what I was doing which to me meant that he enjoyed banging out. I drop my bags and start moving and firing. Dray stands up and dive over a table of roses and flowers running backwards towards Halsey Street. As he reaches Halsey, he turns the corner and disappears.

I jog over to my bag, pick it up and throw the gun in there. I start my bike and pull off making a right down Weirfield St. My mind is racing and I'm saying to myself I have to get off these fucking streets. I head to Dae-Dae's house which is on Hancock and Central. I pull up in front of D's house and yell up to his window screaming, "Yo Dae come down!" Dae comes to the window laughing. I guess he already knew that something had transpired. We knew each other that well until we were able to sense when one of us were in some form of trouble. But nevertheless, Dae rushes downstairs. Come to find out, he had heard the shots from his backyard window. So automatically he knew that it was me in the bang out. I park the bike in his front yard and placed a blanket over it to conceal it, and we head upstairs to his room so I can call a cab. I knew that the police most definitely were looking for those involved in the shootout. Considering it was an old western type of shootout. Thank God no one was hurt. D calls a cab for me, and he straps up, putting his gun in his waist all the while questioning me about the shoot-out. Upset because he wasn't involved. Dae-Dae like myself was a hood thrill seeker and plus shoot-outs against other hood name-brand dudes got us all the notoriety that we thirst for. After maybe ten minutes the cab pulls up in front of Dae's crib and start beeping its car horn. We jump into the cab and head to my mom's crib in Bedford Stuyvesant. The whole time Dae is talking my ears of and questioning me about the shootout. He's asking, did you hit that nigga, what type of gun did he have, why you didn't call me while you were in the store? At that point I just zoned out blocking out D's rhetoric. All I hear is the sound you hear when Charlie Brown's teacher talks about a bunch of nothing. My thoughts are on this meeting tonight with Danny at Junior's restaurant. I'm wondering what could possibly be so important that he wants me to meet him downtown at Juniors and why should I be dressed nice. Anyway, I snap out of my private thoughts due to a sharp elbow to my side. "Man fuck you! You didn't hear a word I said!" I looked at Dae, shook my head no and smiled. He smiled and said, word-to-mother fuck you! And we both started laughing.

The cab finally pulls up in front of my mom's house and she's sitting on the stoop braiding my sister's hair, talking shit with the lady next door named Big Red. Big Red was high yellow, wore a big red afro and red freckles on her face. She had a phat (pretty, hot and tempting) ass, a phat pussy print, and she was in love with me. I just happened to pull up in the middle of their conversation. Big Red is revealing the secret that me and her had been intimate for over a year. She's telling my mom that she's in love with me and that I need to stop fucking with all those young chicks that couldn't do anything for me because a real woman takes care of her man. I walk up and kiss my mom on her cheek, then Dae does the same. Big Red turns to me as though she was anticipating a kiss from me. Instead of a kiss I turn to Red and say "Red why are you out here running your mouth about us? You are a married woman and you're going to fuck around and get your husband smoked if this shit gets out and people start talking. That old nigga's pride is going to get in the way, and he's going to approach me with his nonsense. Red you know that I'm a no-nonsense type of guy!" Dae-Dae looks Red directly in the face and say, "word-to-mother no nonsense baby!" And starts laughing. I turn to Dae and say, "nigga shut up!" I take Red by the hand and pull her into my mom's house and headed straight for my bedroom. All awhile scheming on how I'm going to break her for some cash. My mom already knew what was up.

Once I grabbed Red by the hand because she pretty much taught me the game. How and why, I should break a hoe. She taught me a long time ago that I should be cold, and stomp down on a bitch until she shows me that she is worthy of my love. Until then, make them bitches pay for you! I intended applying every motherfucking principle that my mom had instilled in me when it comes to pimping, hoeing and breaking a bitch. "Make a bitch pay to stay, pay to play if not, send her on her motherfuckin' way!" That's what my momma used to say.

Anyway, as me and Red proceeded to my bedroom, I start shooting game at her, telling her that I had plans for her and me to one day elope and start a life somewhere out of town, but there were some things that I still wanted to accomplish before that could happen. I told her that she had to relax and be patient and then I told her that I understood that she was the best thing for me and that I knew none of these young chicks I was with could ever assist me in all that I was seeking to accomplish. Then I said for example, I'm trying to make a business move tonight with some major players and I'm like a grand short on my half of the investment and still I have no idea where I was going to get the thousand dollars from on such short notice because my team was all out of town hustling. Big Red then grabbed my phallus and said, "don't worry baby I got you." I laid back and closed my eyes as Red pulled out my phallus and pleased herself. In the back of my mind, I'm like fuck JP Morgan I got game! After me and Red's episode, she left and came back with the money. I kissed her on her forehead and told her that I had to get ready for tonight's meeting. She turned away and said, "call me baby."

Anyway, an hour went by, and I had to start getting ready for my big meeting. I went downstairs and told my mother to give me a shape up because my mom was a hell of a Barber. After my mom gave me the shape up, I jumped into the shower. Not five minutes had passed before I hear my mom laughing and yelling from the kitchen, "nigga break me off some of that cash you just broke that bitch for! Your ass is going to catch worms fucking that old bitch!" Dae-Dae repeats what my mom says, "yeah nigga worms!" All along laughing from the kitchen table. I then yell back to them, "my old bitch! My money! They both started laughing.

CHAPTER SIXTEEN
THE MEETING

She was a yellow tone beauty with tiny eyes and black curly hair with a sexy Latin accent. She approached me and asked what I was drinking, and I ordered a virgin pina colada. When she returned with my drink, beside her was Danny. "Boy we all seen when you walked in." Danny said, referring to a group of older gentlemen sitting at a table. The men all nodded and me and Danny proceeded in their direction. When we reached the table, Danny said everybody this is Boogaloo. I looked at him, and he laughed and said, excuse me this is Unique. Danny and I sat down and one of the gentlemen asked me, could I have found anything brighter to wear? Danny interrupted and said, "I told this knucklehead to wear something presentable, and he walks up in here with a bright ass fire man red suit on, with the shoes to match!" The whole table laughs except for me. I didn't find a bit of what they were laughing at funny. I thought I was sharp and dressed to kill. After the men shared jokes about my suit and dress code, one man in particular named Ray said. "That's how them young boys dress nowadays. Hopefully tonight we will change his perception about the game and his loud ass choice of clothing. Within seconds the nature of the meeting changed from jest to strictly business. "Unique do you know what this meeting is about?" Ray asked. "I have no idea." I responded. "Well apparently somebody who's somebody thinks that you have the ability to not be just anybody, but somebody as well. Unique do you understand the purpose of money?" He asked. I was stuck thinking; I didn't want to respond to give the wrong answer and be looked upon as a fool. I had to say something. I said, "to buy the finer things in life and to change your living conditions." Ray looked at me and said, "now how long did it take you to make that shit up or which barbershop did you hear that in?" Then he said, "from this point on I want you to understand that the purpose of money is to make more money! If you keep that up front, you should never ever be one of these broke ass corners standing niggas! But first things first, you must start thinking like the Rothchild's, the Rockefeller's, the Dupont's etc. Then he asked me if I ever heard of economic indicators? I'm like what the fuck is this old ass nigga even talking about! I guess the question was rhetorical because he never stopped speaking. He continued to say some shit about how all market economies regularly go through cycles of recession when output declines and unemployment rises. Then he went on to say that this is when businessmen should be at their best because niggas out of work want to escape the reality of being able to provide. I don't remember exactly what was said, but I know it was somewhere in that area. Back then it all sounded like foreign language to me anyway. But he was pretty much saying that people out of work get high to escape the everyday reality of not being able to provide. Within seconds the tone in his voice went from low to high. Have you ever heard of U.S Bank holding companies such as Chase Manhattan Corporation, JP Morgan & Company, Wells Fargo & Company? Again, it must have been rhetorical because he continued to say.

Well, what we are trying to create is the black dollar. Due to lack of banking and corporate education, we were compelled to make and form our own way of creating business and right now our business is heroin and cocaine.

Ray went on to talk about prohibition and the Kennedy's as in JFK, the 35th President of the United States. How his father was a gangster and a major player in the bootleg game and how he rose to power by selling illegal liquor. He said that if the Kennedy's could do it, why can't we! Ray stopped speaking for about five seconds, then looked at everyone and said, "lethal benevolence baby, lethal benevolence! I couldn't help it, I was inquisitive. I had no idea, so I asked what he meant by, lethal benevolence? He replied, "doing something deadly for goodness!" Ray then motioned for the waitress to come over to our table and we all ordered what we wanted to eat. Them niggas ordered steaks and shit like that and I ordered four Hamburger deluxe and fries. "Damn, your little ass can eat all of that shit!" Ray said. I say "no, it's for my mother, my sister and my homeboy that drove me down here." Danny says, "that's why I like this kid he understands teamwork." I ate my burger and fries, and the waitress packed the other three orders to go. Danny walked me to the door, and on the way out he stopped at the front desk. The waitress handed me a red and white box with a cheesecake in it. Danny says, "Give that to your mom and tell her it's from Ray. I'll be by later this week to tell you what's expected of you!" Danny said. Before leaving, I asked Danny "so my mom knows this guy, Ray?" Danny responds, "no, but Ray knows her." I shook Danny's hand and left. I walk around the corner to where Dae is parked and see him standing at the back of the car taking a piss singing some Jamaican song. When we get in the car, Dae passes me my gun, and we drive to my mother's house. When we arrived back at the crib, before I could put the key in the door, my mother snatched the door open and say, "did Ray send me my fucking cheesecake? That nigga knows how much I love cheesecake!" I say, "ma you know that nigga Ray and how do you know those type of niggas!" She starts laughing and says, "you got Foxy

Brown, then you got Annie White!" She snatches her cheesecake and goes upstairs to her bedroom and shut the door. Now I'm standing in the middle of the living room staring at Dae-Dae all dumbfounded. Dae-Dae says, "man who don't your mother know? Can't you tell how she moves that she stay on her gangster shit!" I'm like whatever and walk into the kitchen, pull a chair from under the table and just sat there staring into space wondering what exactly was my mom into before I was born. Or what was she and Royce into in my younger years.

Anyway, later that week Danny came by my mom's house to sit me down and ran down to me step by step what was expected of me. Basically, I was to take care of their organization's daily functions. I was basically an Urban geographical manager, and you know what that job description entails "brute force." Knowing when to push, knowing when to pull, being able to use diplomacy and all that other shit! After Danny was done running down my responsibilities, I asked him to be honest with me and tell me why and how did him and these guys know my mother so well? Danny said, "boy

I probably shouldn't be doing this, but it's not so much that we know your mother, it's her father who we knew. Your mother's father was a country nigga name Goldie from Williston South Carolina. His mother was a Native Indian, and his father was a popular black man in the South. Your grandfather's father used to make moonshine for all the black people in his town. At first, he started making it as a weekend ritual, and all the black people in his town would come and get a glass or two. Then one day he decided to start selling it and eventually he built a black enterprise business off moonshine because word got out that he had the finest shine in South Carolina. His business had become so big until he started attracting unwanted attention from neighboring towns, such as Aiken and Barnwell County. Apparently, that is where the majority of klansmen lived. Word is that one Sunday while driving his mule and wagon a group of klansmen, un-robed, approached him and tried to make him a business proposal. The proposal was that he needed to consider making them partners in his business, but he refused.

When he refused, one of the klansmen vowed that unless he teamed up with them, his business wouldn't flourish. Word was that my great-grandfather was a cocky, arrogant, strong black man. He told the klansmen, "cracker kiss my ass!" He hit his mule with the whip and pulled off. One of the white men yelled out, "nigga you're dead!" My great- grandfather just kept riding. From what Danny tells me is that my Great-grandfather went home and told his wife what took place. She told him that she hoped he was prepared for what was going to eventually take place. What she meant was that those white men weren't used to blacks being rebellious and standing for their rights in Amerikkka. Or not being feared by them. They deemed blacks such as my Great-grandfather as an uppity nigger that didn't know his place in the white world and niggers like him needed to be dealt with. In their eyesight, the way he moved was extremely irregular and he needed some serious adjustments. My Granddad's pop was no fool! He already knew that he had some unfinished business. So that evening he gathered all his children, and they held a meeting in the woods. My Great-grandfather had eight children, five girls and three boys. There was my Great-Aunt Janie, her sister Sarah Ann, Aunt Ella, Aunt Rosa Lee, and Aunt Moe. Then there was Uncle Bill Bo, Uncle Elco and last but not least, my Granddad Goldie. Goldie at his tender age of maybe thirteen was the meanest of them all. He was always serious and had a rep for being a hell of a fighter in his hometown. Because of his rebellious attitude, he had a gang of followers. Guys such as Ray, and Danny. Goldie and Ray were brothers from other mothers. What they shared most in common, was that they were both the youngest boys of such large families. Ray had nine siblings, so they related to one another quite good. And let's not forget that my Great-grandmother was Indian and so was Ray's mother. So, Grandpa Goldie brought Ray with him to the meeting in the woods, along with Ray's five brothers. My great grandfather informed them that he was going to bring them in as workers of some sort and together they formed an alliance in the moonshine trade. They vowed to die fighting before they allowed those crackers to take their homegrown business. That very same night an alliance was formed. My great Grandfather devised a plan to hide behind the trees when the white klan showed up but, my Grandpa Goldie came up with an even more brilliant plan. He said hiding behind the trees was a great idea but, hiding behind the trees dressed as klansmen was a greater idea. Everybody agreed and said that Grandpa Goldie's plan was great so, my great grandfather formulated his troops. They waited patiently for the klansmen to arrive and for a moment they thought it may have been a false alarm but around two in the morning a few klansmen all dressed in white sheets, led by a chubby built man appeared in front of my great grandparent's house. It was said that they all gathered in the middle of my grandparent's yard yelling "come out you uppity nigger! And if you don't come out, we're coming in to get you!" That's when my aunt Rosa Lee stepped out with a shotgun and shot the chubby man. The loud sound from the shotgun made all the klansmen freeze. They stood there confused because shot came from someone wearing a white sheet. Before they knew it, all my aunts, uncles, Ray and his brothers all step from behind the trees dressed in white sheets firing their guns. Man, the way Danny was telling me this story had me proud to come from such of a bloodline. Now I understood why my mom moved the way she did. She came from a bloodline of fighters so, she had that Nat Turner in her, and I was proud to be of the same stock and bloodline. I became intrigued with this story and the more Danny told me the more I desired to know. Danny explained to me that, what made my grandfather's idea so great was, there was so much logic behind the scenario. For one, having them dress in white sheets was a hell of a tactic. because those klansmen were afraid to fire back not knowing whether they were shooting each other. And two, it made them think that some other neighboring klansmen were down with my great-grandfather so, the plan served its purpose. It was also the last time that my great grandfather was approached on that level. However, as my Great grandpop's business grew, more seasoned white men came pursuing business arrangements. For some time, my great grandfather stood steadfast in his belief that this was his homegrown business and that it should stay amongst the blacks. Again, my grandfather sat down with his father one night at dinner and explained to him the benefits of dealing with the white folks. He explained that by taking the white folks as partners had both economical, and political benefits. My great grandfather agreed and told Grandpa Goldie that he was going to fall back and let him, and Ray run the business. He knew that my Grandpa Goldie was a smart, tough man and he believed in him and his leadership. So, he allowed Grandpa Goldie to run their moonshine business. Immediately my grandpa and Ray called for a sit-down with the neighboring townsmen who were in power. He wanted to meet with them on a professional level and negotiate how they would divide the profits from the neighboring towns. Danny said that this is where Ray was taught that the best businessmen never invest his own money because they were able to utilize the white man's money and political power to take their bootleg business up North. My grandpops had a vision to be bigger than the average Joe from South Carolina.

After maybe five or six years of hard work in the South, Grandpa Goldie and Ray headed North, leaving Aunt Rosa Lee and Uncle Bilbo to run the business. Like so many other hustlers in New York City back then, mostly came from the South. People like the infamous Bumpy Johnson and Frank Lucas were country boys. Back in the days, those country boys came to New York, from South Carolina and some from North Carolina and they meant business. But nevertheless, Grandpa Goldie and Ray took their show on the road. I don't know what quite made them choose Brooklyn NY as their destination, but like most that's where they ended up. For a while they lived on St. Johns Place together which is in the Crown Heights area of Brooklyn. There they immediately opened an after-hour spot selling booze and reefer joints. Inside the after-hour spot they had a pool table, a jukebox and sold dinners. They served collard greens, potato salad, pig's feet, fried chicken and all that good down South food. They even served fried chicken skins. I know it sounds crazy but fried chicken skins drowned in hot sauce is quite delectable.

Anyway, the after-hour spot was a hit for Grandpa Goldie and Ray. They did well enough to purchase a nice piece of real estate in the Bedford Stuyvesant section of Brooklyn. They opened a restaurant on Monroe street and Sumner avenue where they sold hot dogs, hamburgers, and French fries. I also remember they had Italian ice and jars of pickled pig's feet, pickled eggs and pickled hot dogs that sat on the counter. What I didn't know until now is that they sold moonshine, weed and ran illegal numbers as well. I remember Grandpa Goldie had a gay female named Kate running the spot and boy did she love me. Up until today, the true Sumner avenue hustlers still talk about that place.

Excuse me, my mom interrupted. She had come downstairs to tell Danny that his sons were getting impatient. She said she heard someone blowing a horn and looked out of her window. His son asked her to let him know that they were ready. Danny replied, "Shit, I'm their father! I say when we're ready!" With a big smile on his face, revealing his big country gold tooth which most country men wore back then. Danny continued to give me my instructions for what I was to take care of that week. He got up and walked to the middle of the living room and gave my mom a hug. He turned around and slapped me a five and said, now you stay cool like you do and walked out the door. I walked behind him and locked the door.

When I walked back in, my mother was in the kitchen pouring us a glass of soda. She looked at me with a sneaky smirk and said, "what now?" She handed me the glass of soda and walked to the table and pulled out a chair and sat down. She looked at me and smiled. I shook my head because I knew she was about to either drop some type of jewel on me, or in so many words pull my coat to something. Before she started, I sat down and said, "hold on ma, you know that you are an incredible woman and I love you to death." My mom was one of those women who didn't like to show emotion, at least not to me. She drilled in my head that emotions were a weakness for suckers but, I later found out that she was a very emotional woman. Being there wasn't a steady male figure in my life, she was trying to mold me into a strong man. She was taught that strong men didn't display their emotions or feelings. In fact, that's why she wanted me to sit down because she wanted to explain to me that normally a parent would protect their offspring from the likes of Danny and Ray, but I didn't have a normal mother. Her and I were basically born into the game and what was normal to us, was abnormal to squares and we both were far from squares. She said, "boy listen. You're probably asking yourself why I am encouraging you to be a part of whatever it is that Ray and Danny are into? The reality is the truth. Unfortunately, most successful black men in the hood were either drug dealers, pimps, or some type of hustler. The truth is that Ray was once my father's partner, and he is more than a street hustler. Ray is a self-taught businessman. He has business in Real Estate, as well as other legal organizations. Boy I cannot teach you how to be a man. The only thing that I can do is try to mold into the likeness of a man that I respect. Other than Royce, I don't know any other man who can show you the ropes. But you and I both know he will not school you to anything pertaining to the game. Why? Because Royce's perception is totally different from mine. If it was up to him, you would be a square and I know that you are not cut out for that square shit. I figure instead of you getting involved with one of those knucklehead crews, why not encourage you to fuck with a team of official black men who are about their business. Besides, if you didn't know Ray or my father personally, you would assume they were never involved with anything illegal?"

She began to explain the difference between the everyday run of the mill street hustlers, and shrewd businessmen. She said, times had changed and that being a gangster had become fashionable, when the real gangsters hate the fact that they must be gangsters. This was why Ray, and his team wore suits, ties and gator shoes to be able to blend in with top class businessmen. She said that suits and ties gave the appearance of calculating businessmen and the whole objective in the game is to stay below the radar.

I had to give it to my mom, she sounded like she had potential to manage her own team. "Ma they are country boys! I thought them country niggas supposed to be slow." I said, laughing. She said, "nigga make no mistake! That's the first mistake New Yorkers make is underestimating them country boys. Those niggas came up here with a plan and a passion and when you underestimate people you put yourself in the losing position!" I just stared at my mom. I was always intrigued by her when she sat me down and schooled me. She had a way of enlightening me. She then said that her father and Ray were taught and schooled by the infamous Joe. "Who?" I asked. She said, "boy crazy Joe Gallo." "Gallo, are you talking about the dude who made the wine?" I asked. My mom laughed and shook her head. "What's so funny?" I asked. "Ma why are you laughing?" I was still confused and wondered why she thought I was funny.

She then said, "boy I know you're not talking about the Gallo wine guys? Nigga I'm talking about crazy Joe Gallo! Crazy Joe was an Italian gangster from the red hook section of Brooklyn. Joe dealt with a lot of black gangsters which was unusual for an Italian gangster, but Joe was different. Honestly Joe moved different and with more style than a lot of black men. She said that Ray and grandpa Goldie kind of got their dressing style from crazy Joe. I asked her where crazy Joe is nowadays because I would love to meet him! She said boy Joe was murdered in front of Umberto's clam joint on Mulberry Street back in the 70's.

"Wow! Ma Who killed Crazy Joe? I asked. "I have no idea who murdered him. But the word was that an Italian mob did it because he had beef with one of those crime families. Plus, they knew that they had to kill him because Joe started bringing blacks into his organization. Joe was smart, shrewd and he had a vision. It probably would have worked if he would not have been so open with the way he moved. Always remember son, the best attack is a sneak attack! She said. Crazy Joe got too comfortable, slipped up and paid for it with his life!" She said, Joe had control over the jukeboxes, pool tables, pinball machines and he also had his hand in the illegal numbers racket. She also said that Grandpa Goldie and Ray did a lot of business with Joe and that's how they got their jukeboxes. Daddy and Ray were old ass gangsters, and they were connected.

Nigga you're surprised at what your momma knows huh?" She asked.

"Not really Ma, nothing you do or say surprises me anymore." I responded. She went back into talking about crazy Joe. I started getting the feeling that as a young girl my mom had a crush on this white man or maybe she just was infatuated with the lifestyle of gangsters. My mom went on to say that crazy Joe had the characteristics of some acting dudes in those old mobster movies. Guys like Jimmy Cagney or George Raft, but the funny part was that crazy Joe wasn't acting. It was his natural character. She continued to say, that one day Joe came to Grandpa Goldie's restaurant in a fly ass Cadillac. If I could remember correctly, I think she said it was a 1955. She said when he arrived, he had two guys with him. The funny part was that one of the guys with him was a little person (dwarf). My grandfather points, laugh and says, "hey Joe, I see you got your bodyguard with you." The dwarf kicked my grandpop on his knee, then stuck his middle finger up at my grandpa and said, fuck you, Goldie!" When crazy Joe left, she said she asked her

Dad was the dwarf really Joe's bodyguard? My grandpa told her that men like crazy Joe were too proud to walk with bodyguards. He said, Joey was a nut case, and the dwarf was more less Joe's mascot.

After crazy Joe's death my grandpop brought some land down South and built a very nice house. He also opened a mechanic shop, a gas station and an afterhours restaurant.

I remember one day sitting in my grandpop's spot located on Sumner avenue. Kate who was the person who ran his hole in the wall spot got drunk and she started getting loud with her then girlfriend. Kate was not just gay, she was a dyke who wore men suits, gator shoes and packed a 38 pistol. Kate was a hardcore bull-dyker. When Kate got too loud, my grandpop said, "hey man-girl don't make me call up my friends from down on President Street!" He was joking but whenever he mentioned his crazy friends from president street or red hook, people in the spot tended to sober up. Anyway, I always enjoy sitting down talking to my mom.

I say mom listen, "I know that you want what's best for me. That's why you make it your business to guide and school me." "Now there was one man that I would love for you to actually follow. But I know you, and if it's not about a dollar it's going to be a waste of my breathe. Plus, you're not ready." I said, "try me." "Little nigga please!" She said, walking away. "You're definitely not ready for that!" I grabbed the belt to her old raggedy ass house coat, and said "ma who are you talking about?" She then said, "The great Honorable Elijah Muhammad. For some reason I thought that was the funniest shit ever. "Ma are you serious! A fucking Muslim?" "See now, he was a powerful nigga! I told you weren't ready for that." She went to walk upstairs, then said, "and don't get too relaxed, somebody's peeping in the window." "Who is it?" I asked. "Who else?" My mom replied. I looked and damn if it wasn't big Red. We both laughed. My mom stuck up her index finger gesturing that today was the first of the month. Then she whispered to me, "nigga the bitch got her SSI check today. You better let her in, I'm going upstairs. She turned to me again and said,

Elijah Muhammad was a powerful nigga! If you don't know, you better ask somebody!"

Now that I'm older, I sometimes wonder if my mom was a master manipulator because she had a way of getting my attention. For one, just the mention of power drew me to this Elijah Muhammad cat. I was going to have this dude on my mind all day. But first I had to tend to ole girl. Red's purse first, ass last! That was my state of mind. Anyway, after kicking it with red and talking shit. Telling her what she wanted to hear and listening to her complain about ole boy (her husband). I started playing in her hair and pulling her close to me. I then grabbed her by the back of her head, pulled her close to my lips and kissed her on her forehead. "Baby that's what I'm here for." I said. Red was an emotional creature, but women are funny in some ways. Because Red really had a great husband. Her complaint was that he seemed to never have time for her, but the reality was, most good men solemnly have time for their spouse because they are too busy trying to provide for their families. But nevertheless, I was not about to throw an alarm clock in the graveyard to wake the dead. Shit, like big Meech from BMF always say, "if a nigga got time, then he ain't got no money!" Because a nigga who's about his business, time is consumed with chasing money. Broke niggas have all the time in the world because they are not preoccupied with chasing money. Why do you think some broke niggas always end up messing around with some hustling nigga's woman? Because some women don't understand the concept of, "if you work hard today, you can play, relax and enjoy life when you grow old, and the hustle and bustle is all over. Especially if you came from the era I came from! Anyway, after I made Red break herself, (gave me money). I walked her to the front door and told her to come see me tomorrow before I leave town. After Red leaves, I go upstairs. As I reached my mother's room, I heard the smooth relaxing music of Sade and the sweet smell of some Lambs Bread weed.

I smiled to myself and knocked on her room door. "Boy stop knocking on my motherfucking door like you the goddamn police!" She yelled. I started laughing. I could hear my mom laughing from the other side of the door. "Nigga come in!" When I entered, my mom is sitting on the floor playing Atari and my little sister is sitting on my mom's bed eating KFC. My mom had a joint hanging from her mouth with the game controller in her hand, playing frogger. My sister isn't paying me nor my mother any mind. She's too busy eating while my mom is in a serious zone. She's cursing the game out saying shit like "this motherfucking joystick is broke! Who's been fucking with my joystick!" I know exactly who's been fucking with your joystick ma." I said. "Who?" She said. I said, "Bob Marley and snatched the joint from her mouth. I sat on my mom's bed next to my sister and just watched my mom continue to curse and play her Atari. I'm laughing to myself and thinking this woman is special and different. "Ma what's up with this Elijah Muhammad dude? She said, "little nigga not now!" I shook my head and got up to leave the room. As soon as I was about to walk out of the door, she said. "nigga pass me back my damn weed!" For the first time my sister looked up and laughed. She thought it was funny until I stuck my hand in her KFC box and boy did she change her laughter into a cry for help. Screaming, "Ma Unique took a piece of our chicken. My mom paid her no attention, she was way too focused on her game and her weed. I spun around and left my mother's room still wondering, who was this man? and what made him so strong and powerful? As I was going into my room, my mom yelled for me to look on the bookshelf in the living room!" "Why?" I yell back to her. "Come back in here! I'm not going to be yelling back and forth!" I turn back around and walk back into her room. She says, "Message to the Black man in America" is a book by Elijah Muhammad. It's in the bookshelf." "Ma I am not about to read no book!" I said. My mom chucked and said, "well they say if you want to keep something from a nigga put it in a book!" "What's that supposed to mean?" I asked her. She laughed again and said, "nigga when you have some time sit your ass down and check out the book." I walked out of the room and head downstairs. As soon as I reach the living room, I grab the book from the bookshelf and start reading the content. I concluded that my mom was right. I am not ready for this crazy shit but, I embraced it anyway because I wanted to know what my mom found so powerful about this humble ass dude. I soon found out that this man was the strongest, most powerful black man ever, depending on how you define strength, power and wisdom.

Reader Digest once stated that this mild looking man is the most powerful black man in America. He offers a new way of life. Muhammad prompts his severest critics to agree when he says, he attacks traditional reasons why the negro race is weak. But nevertheless, I grab the book, walk outside to my car, and throw it on the passenger side.

CHAPTER SEVENTEEN
SHE CAME THROUGH

I make my way to Dae-Dae's house to pick him and Truth up to ride with me while I made my rounds for Ray. While driving to Dae-Dae's crib my mind drifts to the past events of the week. Especially the conversations I had with my mom and Danny, regarding my new-found responsibilities in the organization. I snap out of my present state of mind because I wasn't paying attention and almost ran a red light crossing Bushwick Avenue. As I approached the light, an unmarked police car was passing. God knows I would have been in a world of trouble because I was packing an army issued colt 45. When I reached Dae's crib, him and Truth are standing outside with stupid smiles on their faces. I'm like what's up with these two stupid motherfuckers. I park in front of Dae's house and as soon as I step out of the car, Dae screams "run nigga!" I didn't take him to be serious because if it was any real beef, they would've gunned down whoever it was. I say to myself these two clowns play too much. That's when Heidi jumped from behind some bushes in Dae's yard and hit me with a two by four wood plank in the center of my back. I fell to my knees and when I stood up, the stupid bitch cracked me in the side. I charged at her to disarm her, then my main girl Cassy stepped from behind the bushes and punch me in my eye. Dae and Truth are now laughing so hard until they are crying. Suddenly, Dae's sister Donna who was just as dangerous as he was, came outside yelling. Man was I happy to see her. "Yo, what the fuck is going on out here! Are you bitches crazy with this bullshit in front of my house!" She screamed. When we looked up on the stairs, Donna is in her brown night gown, holding a nickel plated 357 in her hand. As Donna make her way down the stairs, Cassy and Heidi jumped behind me. I pushed them away and say what's the matter now huh?" Heidi made a dash for it and Cassy calmly walked to my car and opened the passenger side door. "Take me to your house now!" Cassy yelled. Donna came through and put a stop to the madness quick.

Cassy and my mom were crazy tight. In fact, Cass lived with me and my mother on Cooper street before we moved to Bed-Stuy. Cass and Heidi both went to Thomas Jefferson high school and eventually discovered I was dating them both. I didn't really care about Heidi the way I cared for Cassy. Heidi was just a female I enjoyed smoking weed with and sexing. She was a homegirl and a sex partner but, Cassy was my innocent baby. She wasn't a square because she was attracted to bad boys and damn if she didn't pick a true rough neck. When it came to badness, I took pride in being a bad boy. I tell Dae and Truth that I was taking Cassy to my house and to meet me there so we can go take care of our business. Before I left Dae looked at me, laughed and said, "word to mother you pussy!" Before we pulled off, I dug in front of my pants and pulled out my gun. I took the clip out and told Cassy to put the clip in her pocket and place the gun in her waist and she did as she was told. I leaned over and gave her a kiss on her lips. She grabbed my head and stuck her tongue in my mouth and said, "I hate your stupid ass!"

I put in my mom's cassette tape and drove in silence to "Let's stay together" by Al Green.

When I arrived at the house, Dae and Truth were already there standing on the steps talking to my mother, laughing and telling her what happened. When me and Cassy got out of the car, my mom walked over to us and said, "girl I wouldn't have told you that boy was on his way to Dae's house if I knew you were going to go over there and start some shit!" I looked at Dae and we both shook our heads. I guess we were both thinking the same thing. Mom dukes unknowingly set me up. Then Dae said out loud, "Ma word to the mother, you set this nigga up!" Truth started laughing and repeated Dae's favorite line,

"word to mother." My mom embraced Cass and asked if she was okay. Cass shook her head gesturing she was okay and said, "ma Heidi said she knows you. She said the two of you are cool." My mom got straight on defense and said, "girl don't be trying to get me in the middle of y'all shit! That's your job to babysit his dick, not mines!" Then Cassy asked, "but ma do you know her?" My mom responded, "yes I know miss microwave, but you're my baby." My mom and Cass walked in the house, and I went in behind them. I had to get my gun back from Cassy while Truth and Dae waited on the stoop for me to return. When I returned, I went to the driveway on the side of my house and pulled out my motor bike. I pulled out a sock from my back pocket and placed it over my Bally shoe. I told Dae and Truth that our first stop was the Kingston lounge. Truth hopped on the back of Dae's bike, and we pulled off riding like wild outlaw cowboys. The only difference we weren't on horses. We were riding bikes, carrying big guns and on our way to create havoc in crown heights.

When we hit Nostrand and Lafayette, we swing a right and took Nostrand all the way to Atlantic Avenue, made a left on Atlantic, racing towards Kingston Avenue. We pull up in front of the Kingston lounge and decide to walk over to this restaurant Dae loved, called Apache. Apache was a famous Jamaican restaurant where all the hustling Jamaicans frequented. Apache sold fresh baked bread, and a delicious steamed red snapper fish. I used to go there for the Spanglers to pick up one hundred pieces of bread crust, and fifty pieces of fish for the workers and drop it off at the drug spots. When we turned the corner there was a long line of customers. Apache was always busy because as I said, they catered to many of the Jamaican Cartel and their crews. When we approached the spot, a cat name Bigga from the East acknowledged us as we walked up. Bigga kicked my foot in a playing way. "Wah gwaan star?" He asked. Bigga was part owner of Apache and he dug me because I put in some serious work for him on a few fake tough cats who were bullying his son at school. It amazed me how Bigga didn't take no shit, but his son on the hand was soft. But I now understand that sometimes bad boys don't want to turn out their offspring. I walked into the restaurant and Bigga gives me three bottles of Irish Moss, bread crust and fish. As soon as I take a step out of the restaurant, I hear somebody say; "Mi should kick up ya lickle pussy clot!" When I turned around its Betley's black ass standing next to Hines. Hines acknowledges me, Dae and Truth. Yo Yankee dread, tell your boy Chinner me soon come check him!" Chinner was a Jamaican dude who had a weed spot on

Dae's block. Dae says, "Yea Mon!"

I hear Betley say, "Jah know mi don't like dat lickle pussy bwoy!" Hines laughs and says, "the boy Unique is a cool yout! But Betley always had to fuck with me. Hines told him to chill because although I was young, he respected my hustle. Hines also knew in that moment, in front of Dae and Truth I would've had to respond aggressively because Truth and Dae were my little brothers. They looked up to me and I couldn't let nobody punk me in front of them.

"Yo listen, if I ever catch that nigga Betley slipping, I'm going to smoke his ass!" "Word to mother, did you see the fucking name plate he had on?" Dae asked.

"Yeah, if I pop his ass, you can have that shit too! He plays too much!" I said. "Son I don't think he was playing with you. He seems as if he really has a problem with you!" "Yeah, I know. You know the Jamaican chick Tarsha that used to be with your girl Diane?" "Damn does he know?" Truth asked. "Yeah, that's why he hates me, but fuck that nigga!" "Damn!

He got a big ass name plate!" Dae repeats again. I knew what was going through his mind. He was thinking about sticking Betley's bitch ass up. We reached Kingston lounge and I walk in while Dae and Truth waited outside. When I walk in, Ray is sitting in the back at a booth with two other guys. Ray acknowledges me and tells me to cop a seat at the bar. He told the barmaid to fix me a drink and he would be with me in a moment.

She was a sexy little thing, but she was much older. She had on a pair of red leather pants that looked as if they were painted on. To me, she favored the singer Keyshia Cole in the face with a Beyonce body. She had a walk that said, this pussy is good! "What will you have little man?" She asked.

"Little man! There is nothing little about me. If I can, I will have what's in those sexy ass red leather pants." I respond in my best grown man voice. "Ray!!!! She yelled across the bar. Little man is over here flirting with me, and he better watch his mouth before he bites off more than he can handle. He'll mess around and I will send him home to his momma sucking his thumb!" Ray and the two men laughed. "You do know who his momma is? Ray asked her. "No, how am I supposed to know who this young boy momma is Ray?" "That's Annie Jean boy!" Ray said. The barmaid stepped back in shock with one hand over her mouth and the other on her hip.

"Annie Jean! Annie Jean!" She says, enthusiastically." "Yeah Annie Jean!" Ray says. The men at the table all burst out into laughter again. "You mean to tell me old sweet pussy Annie Jean is this boy's momma?" The barmaid asked.

"What did you just say?" I asked, confused. "Alright now Trina!" Ray yelled. This is who you were waiting for. Now take him upstairs and handle business and knock off the bullshit!"

Trina walked from behind the bar and that's when I realized this woman was more than just sexy, she was sex. Not to mention, the way she stood back on her legs, which were extremely bowlegged. I mean, she was a bad older chick.

She stood in front of me, looked me up and down, then poked me in the chest with her index finger and said, "boy follow me!" "Trina!" Ray said. Ray gestured with a wave of his hand for me to follow Trina. He then held up a pen and a piece of paper, pretending to write. "I know Ray! I'm not stupid!" Trina said.

I followed Trina through a door, leading to stairs. "Listen little man, when we get upstairs, I'm going to give you a pen and a piece of paper. If you have any questions pertaining to the business, write it down!" She whispered.

Ray had a no talking business rule in all his establishments which was cool. He barely used the telephone and when he needed to get a message to someone, he usually wrote it down and had it delivered by a trustworthy individual in the organization. One other rule was to always use a payphone away from any of the establishments. Anyway, Trina led me to two apartments where Ray kept his work. Product that was distributed within the five boroughs of New York City. As I continue to follow Trina, my eyes couldn't help but wander back to her ass in those leather pants. Immediately I turned into the atomic dog and my manhood jumps into action, pressing against my pants. As we approached another flight of stairs, Trina turns around, catching me watching her again. She looks down at my pants and starts laughing.

"What's wrong little man, is everything okay?" I had dealt with plenty women, but Trina made me feel uncomfortable and inexperienced. Which was ironic because I considered myself a womanizing cocksman, but somehow intimidated by Trina's sexual prowess. I can't front, at this point my manhood is jumping and I guess Trina sensed my uncomfortableness. She kept turning around seductively smiling as we climbed the stairs. When we reached the top of the stairs, Trina spun me around, pinning me up against a door which led to an apartment. She pressed her tiny hands on my chest and begin kissing me. I begin to shake and realized that for the first time in my life I was intimidated by the opposite sex. Trina reached down and grabbed my manhood. "Why are you so quiet little man?" I didn't respond. Trina had turned me into a speechless little boy. Yet, eager to test those unchartered waters. I'm standing there at a loss for words saying to myself, damn this is a fine sexy bitch. I would love for her to be my secret older women. You know when you're young and growing up, they say you're not really a man until you've dived in some grown woman pussy.

Damn if I wasn't eager to fuck this sexy ass women. Up until now, I had always thought I was in control of my lower desires, but there was something about Miss Trina that was different. Never had I been a sucker for a female but, I have always appreciated fine China and damn if Trina wasn't Fine China. At first, I was kind of intimidated with this sexy piece of ass. Maybe because of the age difference and the fact that I was usually running game on females my age. But this wasn't a young girl. This was a woman at least twenty years my senior. I mean I dealt with women who were a little older before, but not as cocky and confident as Trina. But immediately my momma lessons kicked in. I became pimp-ish and began to aggressively stand in front of her and grab her pussy. She smiled and pushed me to the side. She went in her pocket and pulled out a ring of keys to open the door. She pushed the door open with one hand and grab my hand with other, literally pulling me inside of the apartment trying to take control. As I said before, by then my confidence kicked in and Mack of the year came alive. I flipped the script and grabbed her roughly, spinning her around positioning myself behind her, cupping both of her firm breast and roughly kissed her neck. She then let out a sound of pleasure. I saw the goose bumps as they appeared on her arms. I say to myself, I found her motherfucking spot. Then I turned her around and started sucking on her neck while rubbing on her pussy through her pants. Her eyes began to close as she got lost in enjoying my foreplay. She began breathing hard and licking her own lips. Oh yeah, I got her now. Watch me freak this broad, I say to myself. I continue to turn her on with my foreplay while undressing her sexy

ass. I guess I couldn't get her clothes off fast enough because she began to help me.

"Damn Unique!" Trina said.

"Oh, my name ain't little man no more huh? I responded.

She remained quiet and just stuck her tongue in my mouth as I tore all her fucking clothes off. Unable to control herself she started going crazy clawing at my clothes too. The moment had arrived we were both buck naked. I embraced her and pulled her to the floor on a green carpet. I grabbed a thick pillow from the love seat and placed it under her back. My dick was so fucking hard until it started hurting. It stood up at attention and when I went to lay on top of Trina, she stopped me in my tracks and said, "baby wait." Trina dropped to her knees in front of me and began to give me oral. She was a pro. Never have I had a woman perform oral sex on me like this. Never! She took all of me and had more than a mouthful. She deep throated and caused my toes to bend and curl. I pulled her up by her head, motioning for her to stand up, she complied. I walked her over to the love chair, bent her over and stuck my manhood in her from behind, entering her doggystyle. The juices from her pussy coated my dick, allowing me to slide right in. I don't think she had any dick for quite some time because she winced from the pain before her pussy conformed to my dick. I swear this woman's pussy was magically good. I went deeper and deeper, driving my manhood into Trina. I was enjoying the view of Trina's tight, petite body, and the sound of my nuts slapping against her sexy ass cheeks. Trina started saying, "damn Unique you know this is my dick now!" "Yeah, and you better not give this pussy to anyone else!" I tell her.

"This pussy is all yours little man!" "Little man huh." Trina laughed and said, "it's yours Unique, it's yours!" I flipped Trina in every position imaginable and she couldn't believe my stamina. She'd probably been fucking them older niggas like Ray and them dudes and they couldn't hang with a stallion like Trina. I guess from her experience, young niggas didn't know how to satisfy women because most young niggas were selfish in the bed, but not me. My mom taught me to always make it a night for a woman to remember. I positioned Trina in missionary position on the floor and stuck my manhood back in her and humped like crazy. Trina grabbed my ass and screamed out, "Unique don't pull out! I'm about to come!" I couldn't hold it any longer. I shot my load into her, then collapsed on top of her and we both started laughing.

"You better not give my dick to them young girls" She said. We just laid there for about five minutes. The whole time I'm feeling like superman, giving myself kudos. I couldn't wait to tell Dae and Truth about what transpired. Damn I was feeling myself. Conquering that sweet tail was a notch under my belt. I stood up and began to put my clothes back on. Trina laid there staring at my body as I got dressed. I walked over to a table and grabbed a piece of paper and a pen and wrote down now let's get back to business. I handed the note to Trina, and she didn't waste any more time. She immediately jumped into business mode. She walked her sexy naked ass across the green carpet as if she was Queen of Sheba then she entered the dining room section and opened the fridge. She pulled out two cold beers and handed me one and I handed it back to her. I told her I still had business to handle and that I didn't usually drink while driving or riding motor bikes. She winked her eye and started to a back room returning with a backpack full of dope and coke. In her other hand she held a note that read, Ray said for you to take this backpack to Kings Borough Project. But first you should go to the KFC up the block from Kings Borough on Ralph and Atlantic. There will be a pay phone in front of KFC. You are to beep this number and hang up and within seconds someone should call you back. The person on the other end name is Nice. Tell him that it's Mr. South Carolina and where should you come to meet him. Then tell him to have Stokes come downstairs and bring me my motherfucking money and if he does not have my money, break his under-cover junkie ass up. Don't shoot him just give him an ass whipping he won't forget. Then she handed me another piece of paper which was another note that read, use this like this. She held in her hand a c clamp that plumbers used. She stuck her tiny finger through the c clamp and made a fist. She had turned the c clamp into a pair of hood-made brass knuckles. She looked cute bouncing around like Ali jabbing at the air, then she passed the c clamp to me. Trina kissed me on my lips and rubbed her hand thru my waves messing my hair up. Then she said, "I'll be right back." She stepped in the bathroom, took a quick shower and returned shortly wearing nothing. She picked her clothes up from the floor and got dressed, then we exited the apartment. This time Trina turned her walk up a trillion times sexy. When we entered the door to the Kingston lounge. I noticed Truth and Dae sitting at the bar waiting. I caught Truth tapping Dae to look our way. When Dae spun around he said, "word to mother!" I started laughing and immediately Trina caught onto what Dae was indicating that Trina was a bad bitch. "Yo we out!" I said, as I walked over to Dae and Truth. I turned around and yelled to Ray, "I'm out and don't worry about a thing, it's taken care of!" Ray stood up when Trina turned her back and started stroking the air and laughing, indicating he knew that I fucked Trina. I laughed. Trina walked in front of me, Dae and Truth intentionally wanting them to see her ass. I can't front I wanted them niggas to see what I was dealing with too. Trina walked to the entrance and held the door open for us. Dae and Truth exited first and when I went to exit, she grabbed my hand. She held my hand and whispered in my ear, "here take my number. You better call me Unique and be careful on that motor bike. Don't be driving like a fool." Then she walked back inside staring at me through the glass door. She watched me as I climbed onto my motor bike, and she blew a kiss. I pulled off and Dae followed me.

CHAPTER EIGHTEEN
TREASON

We hit Atlantic Avenue within seconds. Hauling ass, ducking in and out of traffic until we hit Ralph Ave. I took the right and there was KFC. I rode up on the sidewalk and Dae followed. I cut the bike off, made the phone call and Nice called back and told me to meet him at the 4th walk. I jump back on the bike and shot over to Kingsborough projects. When I arrived, Dee Nice was standing with two young men. I pulled up across from him, turned the bike off and Dae did the same. I walked over to Nice and said, "what's up big bro?" I knew Nice was from Downtown Brooklyn. I gave him the bag and he gave it to one of the guys. "Yo, I need to see Stokes!" Nice turned to his soldier and told him to take the bag up and tell Stokes to come downstairs because someone is here to see him. Then Nice started laughing. I asked Nice, "what's funny big bro?" "Ray is losing his mind, getting your little ass to come down here to collect money from

Stokes. What are you 5'6 maybe 5'7 the most." Then he laughed again.

I knew exactly what Nice was trying to insinuate. He didn't know he was just making it worst for Stokes. I intended to break Stokes fucking ass up because apparently, he was under-estimating me when it came to violence. He had no idea how brutal I could be. I said, "as a matter of fact, I'm supposed to collect something from you as well." Nice nodded his head to the other guy standing beside him. The guy handed me a brown paper bag, and I stuck it down in my pants into a jock strap I wore to conceal my gun. Anyway, by now Stokes was coming out of the building with a smirk on his face. I guess he underestimated me too. When Stokes came down the stairs, Dae climbed off the bike and leaned up against a fence. I gave them the eye that I was about to make my move.

"So, you're Stokes huh?" He grinned. I smiled back.

Then I said, "I'm here to pick that thing up for Ray!" He said, "tell Ray to give me a couple of ..." (smash) went the C-clamp against his jaw. He literally screamed. By now Dae has his hands inside of his hoodie jacket pockets and Truth has his hand under his shirt. They're both gripping their pistols. I hit Stokes again and again, by the third time he's laid out on the ground trying to crawl to safety. Now I'm kicking him in his ribs and punching him in the back of his head repeatedly. At this point, Stokes is basically unconscious, but I'm trying to make a statement. And of course, the statement was made. I guess Nice liked the way me and my boys moved because his face tightened and lit up. He was impressed. Then he said, "shit you need to get on the D train! Out with the old and in with the new." I immediately knew what he was getting at. Then he spun around and told his boys to get Stokes off the ground and take him upstairs.

Greed is a motherfucker, especially amongst blacks. One nigga never wants to see the next accomplish anything. We always allow our fucking egotistical and materialistic attitudes to fuck up our plans and intentions. As soon as I met Dee-Nice I sensed he was the type who would do any and everything to get to the top. I think he sensed I was a very analytical cat from our first conversation. I couldn't determine whether he became annoyed with my analysis or whether he was intrigued by my keen sense of thinking and awareness. After Nice seen what I did to Stokes he recognized that me and my crew wasn't your average diddy-boppers and we meant business! After breaking up Stokes and collecting the money we came for, the second job was dropping off the package Nice had given me. Nice put his hands on my shoulder and told me to take a walk with him so he could speak to me in private. My response was, "speak to me about what?" He then gave me a sinister smirk and said nigga just walk. It was more of a command than anything else. As we started to walk off to the side, he began talking.

"Ray told me about you." He said, Ray told him I was before my time and that I honored and respected him. He also said Ray told him I was a special breed. Then he quickly transformed into another person. He bent down and whispered in my ear. "You are on the right track but you're on the wrong train."

Almost immediately I became irritated. I knew exactly where this conversation was about to go. He said, "you need to get off the R train and get on the D train" I shot back, "big bro I don't ride any trains. He smiled and replied, "out with the old and in with the new." At this point I became extremely turned off with Dee-Nice. But I wasn't stupid enough to show my emotions. However, everything Nice was saying to me was basically rhetorical. I mean I was completely turned off. All my life I had been a student of loyalty and honor. While Nice was speaking, I drifted off thinking about the books Danny had given me. Books such as The Prince and The Art of War, just to name a few. I guess Dee really had no real idea of what type of individual he was talking to. I was trained for this shit. Prewarned about treason and divide and conquer. In my short time on this planet, I had already obtained a wealth of information. Both worldly wisdom and intellectual wisdom with a naturally street survival wisdom, which provided me with the code and mannerism of how a nigga should conduct himself in the streets. Treason, treason, treason, I kept repeating to myself. Saying damn now I understand what my mother was telling me about crabs in a bucket. While trying to crawl out of the bucket, the other crabs will reach up and grab the escaping crab's leg and pull him back down. While I'm thinking this to myself, Nice is steadily running his mouth, supposedly shooting game. But I'm unimpressed not merely phased, but he's still shooting his shit. Had he been less interested in his vain ass self he probably would have acknowledged that I really wasn't paying him any attention. But this guy had a taste of wealth, fame and money and that is what usually makes us full of ourselves. So, he kept on going and I kept on thinking to myself. A conversation pops in my head that I had with Royce one night. Royce always pretended as if he didn't know just how deep I was into the streets so I would play along with him. Yet I was always quick to question him about life and the streets. I remember on one occasion I was considering getting into the crack game. I went to Royce and told him I had a friend who was considering getting into the crack game and he said, boy tell your friend to stay away from the crack game. The crack game will only bring a tasteless clientele, and cut-throat friends and partners. Tell your friend to stay away from that shit! He said, crack was at a young nigga exposable, and it didn't really require any brains. The drug game in general was no longer a man's game. Too many young boys are involved at a higher level and they're not too big on thinking and with that in mind you should expect many disputes within your fucking crew and a whole lot of friction from the cops. But most of all greed brings down the new breed of hustlers every time. And eventually the crew falls apart at the motherfucking seams because the mental midgets get fucking greedy and be seeking all the glory. Causing the whole fucking organization to crumble.

He said, boy the streets ain't the same and neither is the game. He went on to speak about the first law of the universe. Stating the first law of the universe was order. Sun -moon -star – kind of like man, woman, and child. Royce always had his philosophical way of getting his point across. He then went on to say that even with legal shit, black people will never really have jack shit. Simply because they aren't willing to accept their role. He said, boy it's hard nowadays because everybody wants the spotlight when they're forgetting the object is to keep the spotlight off their ass.

It was crazy how Royce's conversation was playing back in my head as if he was speaking to me at the moment. I stood there while Dee-Nice continued to talk. He thought I was listening, when I really wasn't paying him any mind. I was caught up in my own thoughts, despising him to the hilt. Royce's conversation is still playing in my head. I'm remembering what he said about everyone wants to be a leader even if they have no idea how to lead. And instead of helping your team in another way they're back biting and trying to disparage the one who's trying to lead. Treason! Motherfucking treason is what I keep repeating to myself and remembering what Ray said. He said, for the crime of treason one should be placed in front of a firing squad and that is exactly where Dee-Nice should be right now. I think it's fucked up Ray thinks highly of this dude and unaware that this guy is praying he falls from grace so he can take his position. I'm thinking to myself as soon as I can get back in contact with Ray, I'm going to tell him about Nice and his deceptive ways. But first, I had to get back to my haven because the stress of the day was beginning to take a toll on me. Plus, Cass was at my house anticipating my return. Me Dae and Truth jumped on our motor bikes and drove down to Atlantic Ave, to Bedford Ave, then down to Lafayette to my mom's house. Once we reach my mom's house, Truth and Dae go to the living room to play some game on my Atari 5200. I can't quite remember but, what I do remember was, my mother yelling, "boy come up to my room when you're finished doing whatever you're doing!" I scream up,

"yeah, ma give me a second."

It was getting kind of late, so I told my homies I was calling it a night. I gave them the keys to my front doors and told them before they crash out if they spark up a blunt to call up to me. Other than that, I was calling it a night. Then my mother yelled down again, "nigga come upstairs!"

I slapped my boys a five and slid upstairs. Before I entered my mom's room I stepped in my room and dug in my pants and pulled out the bag of money I collected for Ray. Then I grabbed the gun from my waistband and placed both the gun and the money in the drawer. I walked over to my bed and kissed the love of my life on her cheek as she slept like a princess in a pair of my BVD underwear. Cass had long jet-black hair that hung down to her ass and it looked like strings of silk on my pillow. She looked so sweet and innocent lying there. Cass was attracted to my bad boy image, but she was a good girl. We were the total opposites and that's what I loved about her. She was young, sweet, innocent, loving, compassionate, and everything I couldn't find in other women. Or maybe I never really gave any other female the chance or the opportunity to express who they really were. I think what attracted me to Cassy was, she always coddled me and spoke words of endearment to me. She was always concerned about my well-being in the streets. I loved her and I was sort of uncomfortable with how she made me feel. All my life my mother taught me to never trust a bitch and that's what was happening to me. I was beginning to not only trust Cass but maybe even falling in love. When I turned around, I noticed my mom standing in the doorway staring at me with tears in her eyes.

"What's wrong ma? How long have you been watching me? I asked. "Come into my room we need to talk." She responded. I waited for my mom to walk out, then I kissed Cass again and went to see my mom wanted. Before entering my mother's room, I had to cut off the lovie-dovie shit, at least that's what I thought. When I entered my mom's room she blurted out, "nigga you know that girl love you right?" I'm confused and saying to myself, what is this a trick question or something. "Unique seriously she honestly loves you and from what I just witnessed; you love her as well." "I like her a lot, but I don't know about the love shit." Then I went on to say, "you do know that I know love is a counterfeit emotion for suckers." She immediately shot back, "nigga shut the fuck up! I don't want to hear that pimp shit right now I'm speaking from the heart. Cass loves you and she also has your best interest at heart, and nigga you feel the same! I know I taught you to always keep your guards up when dealing with women, but Unique I swear this one is special. Momma won't steer you wrong!" I left on that note and went downstairs to shower before I jumped in the bed with Cass. Truth was still up playing the Atari and eating a hero sandwich from the Arab store on Bedford Ave. Suddenly Dae said out loud, "nigga shut up I don't want to hear that pimp shit!" And him and Truth both burst out laughing. Then he said, "say word to the mother this bitch ass nigga is in love." Then Truth started singing Marvin Gaye (Let's get it on). "There's nothing wrong with me loving you, baby no no and giving yourself to me could never be wrong if the love is true, oh baby." Dae burst out laughing. What happened was those two fuckers were eavesdropping on me and my mother's conversation. As dangerous as we all were, we were equally funny. We all had a clown streak in each of us. Truth made me laugh because the song he chose to sing was his mother and father's favorite song, and it was also my Grandparents' favorite. At every cook-out my Grandparents and Truth's parents would jump up every time the song came on. Our families and the neighborhood DJ Tubby played it intentionally at every cookout. That's why Truth sung this song because me and Truth were raised together as family, and it was basically a private joke. But the reality was, I was beyond falling in love with Cassy, I was in love with her. I hid my feelings because I was conditioned to protect my heart. Growing up, I observed all the crazy shit my mom did and how she dealt with men so, I know anything is possible when it comes to women. Plus, my mom also told me out of her mouth I should never trust anything that bleeds for seven days! Anyway, after taking a shower I went back upstairs and laid next to Cass and cuddled up next to her. Once she realized I was in bed with her, she wrapped her legs and arms around me and kissed me on the cheek. Then said, "I was worried about you Unique. You scared me baby!" "There's no need to worry about me. I'm safe like money in the bank baby." I wrapped my arms around Cass and drifted off to sleep.

CHAPTER NINETEEN
RAPTURE OF LOVE

First thing in the morning, I awoke to the smell of breakfast. Cassy and my mom were downstairs cooking for me Dae, Truth and my little sister. Meanwhile I'm waiting upstairs in my room for Cass to return with my breakfast, thinking to myself, is it love? Could my mother be correct? If I'm capable of loving someone, should I allow myself to be vulnerable and carefree?

Is my mother a hypocrite? She's now telling me something totally different from what she taught me as far as I can remember. Whatever happened to "(don't trust nothing that bleeds for seven days and don't die). And "(nigga what's your malfunction, don't you know it was Eve who tricked Adam into eating the forbidden fruit, now the world has been fucked up ever since). Or was all that just a play to strengthen me in what she perceived as manhood? Damn I need to do some self-evaluation because shit is affecting me both internally and externally. Damn I wish my father was in my life, to at least school me in this field. As soon as I get out of this bed and hit the streets, I'm going to see Royce. Royce has always given me some form of structure and counseled me without pulling any punches. Yeah, that's what I'll do, go kick it with Royce. Or maybe Ray can give me some insight on this matter. Or maybe I'll go holla at Danny. Shit I don't know what I should do. Mama never steered me wrong before and she had tears in her eyes. Shit, I got the game from my mother. My mother is the one who encouraged me to fight back when I came home with a black eye. She taught me how to throw a jab, and she also taught me how to be a leader. She's the one who taught me how to dictate policy since as far as I can remember. She has always cared for me. She gave me food, clothing and shelter. She nurtured me while I was in her womb and cared for me when I exited her womb. I remember when I had Chickenpox, she rubbed my entire body down with lotion three or four times a day. I remember when I was sick, and my nose was running with mucus, she would literally suck the mucus out of my nose using her own mouth. That's some shit only a mother can do.

Maybe she does have my best interest at heart, but I'm still going to see Royce and get a man's perspective on this love shit. I hope I'm not going soft. Is it even manly to submit to this love shit? Does it make me less than a man? I don't know maybe I'll just go with the flow, but right now I'm confused!!! I'm a gangster and gangster's make the rules so if that's the case maybe It's okay to love, even if only for the moment. Damn where's my pops? Damn I'm confused, really fucking confused.

CHAPTER TWENTY

HE THAT IS NOT WITH ME IS AGAINST ME

Mathew 12:30 KJV

"Hey Ray, we need to talk." Is the first thing I say as I enter the Kingston Lounge. Ray is sitting in the back of the lounge caressing a glass of liquor. Whatever he was drinking looked rather classy. A slice of lime and olive adorned the glass with two pieces of ice. Ray held the glass with his right hand and rubbed his index finger around the brim of the glass in a circular motion. Ray always displayed some form of class and sophistication. I admired Ray and I occasionally tried to mimic his every move. But nevertheless, I walk to the back of the lounge where Ray is sitting with two other gentlemen. Ray says, "have a seat Unique." I take a seat next to Ray and ask him, "Are we okay?" He responds, "yes they're family." I then dug in my jock strap and pulled out a brown paper bag of money I collected from Nice the day before.

"Can we talk Ray?" I asked.

"Unique you are around family, it's okay to say whatever you please." I looked him in his eyes and said, "Ray do you trust Nice?" "Why Unique?" He responded. "Ray everything you told me about deception and treason, I somehow sense those qualities in Nice." The man to the left of Ray named was Bubby and the other name was Hornet. They both shook their heads in agreement, not in agreement with me, but in agreement with Ray. Ray just had a conversation with them regarding Dee-Nice over his ambitious desire to eagerly climb the ladder of success. Ray was sure Nice would try to cleverly induct me into his crew, especially after he saw how I viciously handled Stokes. Ray knew that Nice thrived off implementing fear and brutally enforcing it by any means. He also felt as though I would have been an asset to his organization. However, Ray was carefully grooming Nice to become the heir to his throne and Nice was only following Ray's orders. It was Ray's slogan Dee-Nice utilized when he said, "out with the old and in with the new!" Ray's plan was to bow out gracefully and let Dee-Nice take over his organization.

The era of shrewd businessmen was over. The era of coke and dope was still in effect but, the world was not prepared for what the government had planned for us.

The era of the "New Jack Hustler" was on its way. The infamous crack era and in order to control and flourish in the game, one had to possess two qualities. To be extremely shrewd and vicious, and damn if Nice wasn't equally shrewd and dangerous. So, he was a prime candidate for becoming the heir to the throne. Ray explained to me that Nice wasn't trying to betray him he was respectfully and earnestly doing as he was recommended to do. Ray said, he had just told Bubby and Hornet that my loyalty was with him, and I would probably take offense to Nice trying to recruit me. Especially since I knew the history of him and my grandfather. Ray then grabbed me in the headlock and said, "Unique never lose that quality, because loyalty should only be given to those deserving. But never misinterpret loyalty for stupidity. Because in the hood where we become ghetto stars, and hood politician, political understanding and consideration is paramount. I admire the fact that you understand shit like this at such an early age because lack of loyalty and treason is the ultimate way to paralyze a team every time. But for the record, Nice isn't guilty of treason. In fact, I suggested he may want to consider incorporating you in his organization. You understand?" "Yeah, I understand big bro. Honestly, what none of us understood or will ever understand, is what the future had in store for us. The crack era. We didn't see it coming! We had no idea whatsoever how our whole generation would be altered and destroyed thirty years later. Some people are still trying to recover from the crack era. Isn't that a bitch?

In the Holy Qur'an
Surah Al-Baqarah 2:219

They ask you about wine and gambling. Say, "in both there is a great sin, and some benefits for the people. but the sin of them is greater than their benefit.

CHAPTER TWENTY-ONE
WELCOME TO THE CRACK ERA

"I came in the door, bet you can't endure, never let crack magnetize you no more. It's slighting you, and biting, it's fighting you to smoke. Smoking on that shit ain't no motherfucking joke!"
Remix-Unique
Eric B and Rakim - Eric B for President

The thumping sound of loud music blaring from customized European cars. Cars like BMW and Mercedes Benz ripped up and down the streets playing songs like, Eric B for President, La Di Da Di and The Show. Everybody who was in the game wanted to be seen and heard. The days of staying beneath police radar was a thing of the past. It was all about glitter, flash and notoriety. No longer were rap groups and R&B singers the entertaining icons for our young black generation. Our entertainers were replaced with diabolical, uneducated, once poverty stricken, young, egotistical, drug dealing, psychopathic, unorganized, black and Latin youth who had no perception of what order was. The only things they knew were violence and brute force. The only requirement was being able to sustain from the usage of drug. Most of the drug dealers of the crack era had lower than a public Jr. high school education. Some were in the range of a sixth and seventh grade education and common sense was a non-existing factor. The crack era produced such notorious men. Movies such as New Jack City and King of New York were based on the lives of such men. Men who ruled the streets with an iron fist with no regards for the police and its corrupted establishment. Our once community-oriented neighborhoods became battle zones, as vicious drug lords gunned each other down for territory. It became a common occurrence to hear guns being fired at nine o clock in the morning, while sitting at the table eating breakfast with your family. Gun shots were so common until we became immune to the sounds of screams and big guns being fired off.

It became the norm, which was rather sad because so many people lost their lives all in the name of money, power and respect. And the sad thing was, none of us really had an idea of what money, power and respect meant. Our only analogy of it was a motion picture that hit the movie theaters sometime in the early eighties, 1983 to be exact. The title of the movie was "Scar Face." Al Pacino played the character of a poor Cuban illegal immigrant who migrated to Miami from Cuba after Fidel Castro opened the prisons and released Cuban convicted felons. The movie Scarface gave us young, poor, Black and Latin Americans hope. We felt, if a poor Cuban immigrant could come to America with nothing other than the clothes on his back, climb out of a barrel of despair and achieve some degree of financial stability, then it was possible for us young Black and Hispanics to achieve the same. Especially since most of us were born here on American soil. It gave us the belief that we could easily climb the ladder of success, and out of the extreme clutches of poverty, and into the light of prosperity. That movie helped shape, construct, and mold the mentality of the youth of that era. It gave us a false economic blueprint that was so far from the truth. But in those uncertain times there was an obvious need for us to believe in something and we chose to venture into the drug trade. Although the drug trade was new to most young men my age, I had already been prepped and exposed to the game since the early seventies because of my family's background. My grandmother and step-grandfather were the neighborhood bootleggers, and I would usually have to serve their customers when they were busy serving someone else. So, to avoid the house getting too crowded I had to assist them. I was prepared as a youth to be a hustler of some sort. And as I mentioned earlier, my mom's father, Goldie White was also involved with the drug trade. Selling weed, heroin and cocaine in the Bedford Stuyvesant area of Brooklyn. Although back then the hustler's tended to stay beneath the radar, their families usually were involved to some degree. They implicated their families so they could keep their circle tight because they didn't want outsiders involved with their business.

This was one of the many tactics the old hustlers used to stay beneath the radar. Besides hustling, back then it was considered a homegrown business because that's all they had. Unlike today's hustlers, they came from the South to New York. They came to build a legitimate foundation for themselves and their families. It was done to make illegal money legal so they could create some form of revenue. Creating legitimacy was their ultimate goal. It wasn't to flash and floss (attract attention) but, those days were now over. And although I was taught by the best I performed recklessly. If not even more reckless than the new jack hustlers, which was sad coming from a leader such as myself. But like I said times had changed and in order to survive and thrive in the game, one had to be ruthless yet cunning and shrewd. It was pure insanity, kind of like a double edge sword. But in the mist of it all, I was playing my part in contributing to the demise of my race. Total insanity.

"Motherfucker where's your bitch ass brother?" I

yelled out to a dude whose brother ran off with some work that was given to him by Trina. Trina usually took a little extra work from Ray's stash house to make extra money. And because I was secretly fucking Trina, I basically became her enforcer. When people had a problem paying Trina for work (drugs) she fronted them, I would take on the responsibility of collecting for her. It wasn't that I was working for Trina but, by this time Trina and I were deeply involved physically and spent a lot of time together. Basically, we were sort of an item and what was Trina's was essentially mine. So, damn if I was going to let anybody play Trina by not paying her for what she gave them on consignment. That would be allowing someone to take food out of my mouth and I wasn't going for that shit! Anyway, the fiend didn't see me and Dae pull up on him in Trina's Buick as he were exiting the Burger King's parking lot on Kingston and Fulton. Dae spots the fiend first. "Unique ain't that Harry's fiend ass brother right there?"

Harry was the dude's name who ran off with Trina's work. "Yeah, that's his bitch ass!"

It's around 9:30pm and the streets are still crowded because Kingston Ave. and Fulton Str. was a busy Urban shopping area. People were still out so we had to be careful how we approached Harry's brother. Instead of confronting him on Kingston and Fulton we followed him for two blocks until he went down a side block. Once he made the turn down the block, I told Dae to turn off the head lights and ease up on his chump ass so we can catch him off guard. Dae turns off headlights and I rolled the window down to the passenger side of the car door and lean my upper body out of the window with my gun in my hand pointing at Harry's brother. He never noticed he was being followed. He never saw it coming until he was staring down the barrel of my gun. When he turned around, he froze for a minute then motioned to run. "Nigga if you move as much as a muscle, I'll paint the concrete red with your blood. Dae-Dae got out and came around to the passenger side of the car with his gun pointed at Harry's brother to make sure he didn't move. I then get out of the car and walk up to him and immediately slap him with my pistol and told him to get in the passenger seat of the car. I climbed into the back seat with my gun still pointed at him and Dae gets back in behind the wheel, start the car, and pulls off. Harry's brother assumes his life is over. However, that's not the plan because dead motherfuckers can't pay debts but as far as he knew his ass was as good as dead. I slapped him in the back of his head and ask him where was his brother? Almost immediately he gives up the location and tell us he is located on Putnam and Nostrand at his drug spot. I asked him who was at the drug spot and does his brother have security? He says, there's no security. It's just his brother, a lady and her kids who live in the apartment he used to sell his drugs. Back then, it was common for a drug dealer to take over a person's apartment who was addicted to drugs. Especially crack cocaine, and that's exactly what Harry had done. He took advantage of the lady's addiction and paid her a few cracks to use her apartment to solicit his drugs and occasionally use her as a sex slave. Making her perform degrading sexual acts for crack cocaine. I despised drug dealers who committed such acts. Taking advantage of people who unfortunately fell victim.

On our ride to Harry's spot, his fiend ass brother told us how much he disliked his brother because he had turned him on to crack cocaine. He said, the apartment Harry used was his and his wife's apartment. The woman was Harry's sister in-law, and the two kids were his children. He said, he hated how his own brother could make his own sister-in-law perform degrading sexual acts for crack. The more Harry's brother expressed his deepest sentiments, the more anger aroused in me. This only added fuel to the fire that burned inside of me. I couldn't wait to break this chump ass nigga up because I saw Harry's type before.

Crack cocaine somehow made this weak ass coward God. I hated motherfuckers like him.

My mind drifted off to a time when I saw a drug dealing, bitch ass, part time homo thug ass nigga, fuck this dude up his ass. The dude was once a notorious stick-up kid who was addicted to heroin, then he graduated to crack. Such a sad thing to witness. But nevertheless, I didn't really lose any respect for the guy who was getting fucked. I lost respect for the chump who stuck his dick up that man's ass. I mean both of their morals were warped, but one was under the influence of drugs and the other was just outright sick in the fucking head. But that's what crack cocaine had the tendency to do, it made the strong, weak. And the weak, strong. But nevertheless, the thought of what this coward was doing had my temperature rising at a high velocity now. I was anticipating getting a hold of this nigga. I myself had some anger issues I needed to address. But for now, I was going to use his bitch ass as a punching bag and release some stress by working his bitch ass over. When we pulled up to Harry's brother house, we see Harry's burgundy and grey two-tone deuce and a quarter Buick sitting in front of the crib. I must admit Harry's car was looking type fly. Shit I even considered taking his car for collateral if he didn't have Trina's money. We pulled up and parked, but before exiting the vehicle, I told Harry's brother this situation wasn't personal, and just business. Nothing more, nothing less. I wasn't apologizing for the aggression I displayed because it was an unwritten policy in this business. Basically, my behavior was standard procedure for one in my position. I had to use force in order to maintain control in such a business. The crack game was so fucking unpredictable. One mistake could be extremely vital.

That one mistake could be your last mistake so you would never want to give anybody the impression you cared. Such sentiment was strictly forbidden. Anyway, we sat in the car for a couple more seconds for security reasons. I wanted to peep the scenery to make sure Harry's brother wasn't trying to set me up. I also let him know what the consequence would be if that was his plan. After giving him a quick lecture on the possibility of him getting his ass marked, we then proceeded to exit the car and head inside. Harry brother's family lived on the second floor of a three-story brownstone building which sat in the middle of the block. Upon entering the building, you couldn't help but notice that this particular property was once a nice piece of real estate. But the traffic from all the crack head customers who frequented the building, started to take a toll on its condition. The building had begun to deteriorate. The once expensive brownstone was on its way to becoming a sad eye sore. The once beautiful parquet floors were now covered with crack valves and empty bottles of beer and cigarette buts. As me, Dae and Harry's brother climbed the stairs we see a black female to the left of us performing oral sex on a kid who couldn't had been no more than ten or eleven years of age. The female was at least forty years his senior. She was old enough to have been this kid's grandmother. I can still remember how this woman looked. I guess her crack addiction hadn't caught up to her yet because she still was fine as all outdoors. She still had a beautiful shape but the one thing that stood out the most about this woman was her Betty Boop spandex body suit and her blond hair which was crazy considering she was a black woman. I mean jet black. She had to be of west Indian descent because when Harry's brother said, "Cookie, bitch you should be ashamed of yourself sucking that little boy's dick every fucking day." She responded with, "mudda cunt!" But when she finally came up for air from sucking the little boys dick. She noticed the guns me and Dae had in our hands. Her cockiness was replaced with a terrified scream. But Harry's brother informed her to shut the fuck up and she went back to business as if she never seen the guns. As crazy as it may seem, a lot of guys lost their virginity to a crack addict female or even a male crackhead who were willing to do something strange for some change. I'm telling you that crack shit was a coldblooded motherfucker. Anyway, as we approached the door, I hear voices screaming and yelling on the other side of the door to the apartment we were about to enter. An all too familiar voice said bitch, "I ain't giving you shit for free!" Then I heard a women's voice say, "everything you give me is due to me. Did you forget about our agreement Harry?" "I tell you what if you do that trick for me again, I'll throw you a little something something." Harry says. His sister-in-law says, "Harry why must you constantly blatantly disrespect me in front of my kids?" Then Harry says, "How about drinking my kids." He starts laughing like he really said something slick and funny. I didn't find what he said a bit funny. I told his brother, "man put the key in the door so we can enter the crib." He said, his keys didn't work because Harry has a two by four braced up behind the door. "I have to knock on my own door and then pray he allows me to enter." Me and Dae stood on both sides of the door, out of view so that Harry wouldn't know his brother had company with him. He knocks on the door. I guess they shared some secret knocking code because Harry's brother knocked four times and Harry knocked back two times responding to his brother's knock.

"Stop knocking on the door like you're the fucking police or the feds or somebody!" Harry yells. Harry's brother humbles himself and says, "man I'm tired like a mother fucker, besides I have a couple of hundred I came across and I want to spend it with you. Come on man open the door!" Then you hear his son yell out to his sister, "Sherry daddy's home!" It was obvious that, although their father was a crackhead, those children still loved their father. You could hear how overwhelmed these kids were after hearing their father's voce. Harry screams at the kids and tells the boy to get the fuck away from the got damn door before I slap your punk ass down!" Then you hear the door unlock. As soon as the door opened, me and Dae slid instantaneously into the apartment with our guns drawn. Harry froze symbolically like a deer froze stuck at the view of an automobile's head lights. I rose my gun above Harry's head and came down on the middle of his head with the butt of my gun. Dae followed with a slap to his jaw with the side of his gun connecting with Harry's jaw. Blood mixed with saliva went flying from his mouth. The sound of Harry's jaw breaking was almost deafening. Harry dropped to the floor like a sack of potatoes and let out a scream as he curled up like a cheese doodle in a fetal position. He screamed out "Unique please don't kill me I got Trina's money please man don't kill me please!" The once cocky, arrogant, belligerent man was now passive and unaggressive and extremely submissive as a mother fucker begging for his life. I kicked him in his gut and told him to stand up. As Harry begin to stand up Dae swiftly kicked him again and Harry fell back to the floor. I reached down and pulled him back up to his feet pointing the pistol to his temple and asked, "where's my bitch bread?" Harry says, "man I have her money." I followed Harry to the room he occupied and stashed his money and drugs. The room was so immaculately kept, it looked like a whole different place from the other rooms in the apartment. The apartment wasn't filthy, in fact it was equally clean. However, there was no furniture in the other half of the apartment where Harry's brother, wife and kids occupied. I'm sure it was due to Harry's brother and sister-in-law crack addiction. They didn't have any furniture or anything worth value. Probably because they sold any and everything that was worth something. In the room Harry occupied, there was a bar, a floor model television set, a nice size record player, and a camcorder. The camcorder was hooked up to his television set because Harry occasionally taped him and his sister-in-law's sexual acts. Harry had his stash of money and crack hidden in the floor. He had the floor model television set placed over the secret hole in the floor. He pushes the television to the side and bingo there it was, an abundance of money and crack. I immediately called Harry's fiend brother to the room and told him to bring me a bag because there was more money than we had anticipated. But when Harry's brother entered the room, his wife followed. She stood behind her husband with a smile on her face so radiant, it could have lit up a house where Con-Ed had shut off their lights for nonpayment. She was overwhelmed because the man who degraded her daily was now crunched up in a corner pleading for his life. She looked over at Harry cowering on the floor and said, "ya ain't so tough now huh?" I told her to be quiet and leave the room. She then says, "he's not being honest with you guys he has a safe in his walk-in closet as well." I immediately looked at Harry and noticed the tears rolling down his face. I motioned for Dae to go check it out and once Dae entered the closet I heard him scream out at the top of his voice. "Say word to the mother this nigga got bread!" It was just our luck this nigga had his safe wide open. I told Dae and Harry's sister-in-law to go inside and clean that motherfucking safe out! She shot pass Dae in a rush in hopes of pocketing some extra cash for herself, not knowing that I had intended on blessing her lovely with cash and drugs for pulling our coats to the big stash in his walk-in closet. Thanks to her, we were more than compensated for what Harry owed Trina. Plus, I kind of felt like she deserved to be compensated for the humiliation she endured from Harry due to her crack addiction. She was unaware of the catch twenty-two. Harry's spot was now about to be under new management!

Two weeks later in front of Trina's crib in Lindsay Co-op while waiting for Trina to come downstairs, two mask men drove up in a green Cadillac Seville and took multiple shots at me. I immediately ducked behind a car and pulled out my colt forty-five from my waist and to took aim. They quickly pulled off heading down Broadway with the attempt on my life. Unsuccessfully taking shots at my adversaries in the Caddy I noticed a young kid on a BMX bike coming towards me with a pistol in his hand aiming my way. I'm like damn these niggas are trying to off me for real and they sent a child to finish the job. Again, I took aim at the little boy. I didn't want to kill shorty, but I had to let him know that I wasn't the nigga to mess with. When he saw that I was not playing with him, he then jumped off the bike and took flight. I chased him through Lindsay co-ops parking. The little bastard spun around and fired like five shots in my direction. He shattered a bunch of car windows but missed me completely and disappeared around the corner, but I continued to give chase. As I turned the corner shorty reappeared taking aim at my head. I braced myself anticipating death. Shorty took aim and everything seemed to slow down. My whole life appeared before me, and I suddenly realized that my life on this planet was rather short. It's amazing how things you take for granted just seconds ago, become so important when you're confronted with death or at least the thought of death. I closed my eyes, expecting for that to be the last time. Shorty squeezed the trigger, but nothing came out. I opened my eyes and saw shorty jump in the green Cadillac Seville that had just took shots at me seconds ago. As the car pulled off, I stood there motionless with my gun dangling from my hand in a state of shock. My breathing became deeper and deeper. My legs became heavy, I couldn't move and just stood there. Not knowing what to do. My fucking legs felt as if they were made of lead and my heart was jumping around in my chest. I had to force myself to snap back to reality. The adrenaline that pumped through me, overwhelmed me to the point as where my hands were shaking. Suddenly, out of nowhere I begun to laugh. Life was crazy like that. Did I want to secretly die? Or did I find flirting with death almost erotic or orgasmic? I became erect from the near-death experience. In reality, it was just another day at the office. Just another day in the hood.

I couldn't wait to tell Dae what happened to me.

Later that week another attempt was taken on my life. Only this time I was walking out of a sea food restaurant on Emmons Ave in Sheepshead Bay Brooklyn. I took my main lady Cassy out to eat. I'm not quite sure whether the restaurant was Randazzo or Lenny's. I was really upset about this situation, because Cassy was the love of my life, and she was innocent. As far as I was concerned, she was only guilty of dating a gangster. I was filled with rage. How dare these mother fuckers try to off me in front of my Latina princess. Somebody had to die! That's what I'm thinking but, the sad part was that I had the slightest idea where to begin looking for my foe! I had accumulated so much beef that it could have been anybody trying to take me out. I grew over cautious about every move I made. The word paranoid was an understatement.

Almost immediately I went and brought myself a bullet proof vest and an extra gun. I swore that if anybody approached me sideways, I would shoot and ask questions later. Paranoia became survival instincts for me.

Later that week I was back at Trina's crib. I loved spending time at Trina's. It had wall to wall pure white carpet. White as the driven snow. When entering Trina's apartment, you had to take off your shoes and put on a pair of slippers. In the middle of Trina's living room, she had a Classic Grand Piano. The type that Beethoven played. The Piano was pure white with black piping around its edge, and it was beautiful. Expensive paintings of African men and women adorned her walls. She had lacquered black and white shelves on the wall that held fine African artifacts. A crystal chandelier hung from the ceiling directly over the Piano. In each corner of Trina's living room there were tall black African statues with big ass noses, fat asses and great tits on them. I made a habit of rubbing the breast of the statue by the terrace entrance whenever me and Trina went out on the terrace for our occasional glass of champagne and our weed escapade. We ate dinner on the terrace sometimes too. Trina was a great cook. We would smoke, sip champagne and then eat a delicious plate of food. Sometimes just sit on the terrace cuddling and French kissing appreciating each other's company. Then at times things got rather heated especially after Trina got some damn Champagne in her system. She usually drank this brand name Piper Heidsieck and it turned her into a crazy ass sex maniac. She would begin placing sloppy wet kisses all over my face. She would start sucking on my earlobe with her hot ass alcohol breath. I was always eager to accept her tongue into my mouth. After moments of kissing, Trina's alcohol tasting tongue would turn into the sweet taste of nectar. Trina would climb on top of me as I sat on the white custom-made love seats she had on the terrace and just have her way with me.

Trina was a professional when it came to oral sex, and she had a way of making my toes curl. As I sat in the chair, Trina would just start sucking on my lips and neck, working her way down to my chest. Although my chest was as flat as a white woman's ass that didn't stop Trina. She would drop to her knees and take my manhood into her mouth and send me straight to ecstasy right there on the terrace. I would always pull her up off her knees, take her panties off and bend her over the terrace railing. Trina had the prettiest shaped ass I had ever seen, and I enjoyed taking control of her from behind. I loved the way Trina responded to my sexy bad boy antic. In fact, I think she was more turned on with the fact that she still had what it took to pull a young, up and coming gangster who had some street cred and was both fly and feared in the streets. All of that combined with the fact that I laid my sex game down. Our sex-capade always started out on the terrace but ended up in Trina's bedroom. Her bedroom was a love nest. The color of Trina's bedroom was fire truck red. Trina invested a lot of money into the decor. She personalized and beautified everything in her room. She even went as far as customizing her bed. Trina's bed was built into a giant shaped heart. You had to climb three steps to get on her bed. The bed was made of black siding at the very bottom and the other half was also fire truck red. She had silk bed sheets and silk pillow covers. This female had class and taste and was sexy about it. Her bedroom also had decorative elements such as wall sculptures, sconces, framed artwork and personalized pictures of us. My lady was elegant, and I was more than eager to wrestle in the sack with her. Trina introduced me to a certain lifestyle that was foreign to most men my age. Shit, most men in general. Years later I found out that Trina was Ray's mistress at some point in his life and he still took care of her as a result of her loyalty and honor. Predominately, Trina was her own woman and stood on her own two feet. Ray just allowed her access to drugs in abundance, and she took advantage of the opportunity. Unlike most black women back then, Trina didn't really rely on a man to take care of her. She made her own bones. Trina was so important in Ray's organization, that she even had access to the safe in Ray's stash crib which allowed her to live this extravagant lifestyle. The safe that Ray kept in the stash house had a digital clock built into the vault so if anyone attempted to open it, Ray would be alerted immediately. Which was cool because Trina always called him ahead of time to inform him, she was about to go into the deep freezer to cook dinner. Anyway, that's what she called the safe.

I was living the life so of course I grew fond of Trina and the trappings that came along with being her young sex toy and enforcer! I wasn't in love with Trina, but I was in love with the lifestyle she had to offer me, so I spent a lot of time with her. Trina acknowledged our time together as quality time. But in all honesty the time I spent with Cassy was quality time for me. The time I spent with Trina was basically business that came with the territory of success plus uninhibited sex. Trina had no sex hang ups at all. She was a super freak and I often wished I was able to provide Cass with the lifestyle Trina provided for me. I was stuck between a hard place and a rock. I was in love with Cassy, but I was also in love with the luxuries that dealing with Trina had to offer me. And damn if I was willing to lose either one of them so I just let it play itself out. I just went with the flow.

CHAPTER TWENTY-TWO
PARANOID

As I turned the corner, I noticed two hooded men following me. I step up my pace in hopes of eluding the two hooded men. As I put more pep in my step, the predators began to move in. As I approached the corner of Tompkins and Putnam Avenues, two more hooded men quickly turned the corner with two automatic machine guns in their hands aiming directly at me. I froze unable to move a muscle then suddenly, four armed killers were aiming and squeezing the triggers of their machine guns. The bullets entered and exiting my body. I saw my own flesh as it hit the pavement and smelled the smoke coming from my open wombs. Then one of the gun men pointed his machine gun at my head. I closed my eyes and screamed like a little bitch. Instinctively Cass woke up. I had wakened her from the nightmare I was experiencing. My abstract lifestyle was taking a heavy toll on me. Mentally physically and emotionally. And not only was it starting to affect me, but it was starting to affect those around me. Damn the demons that I tried so hard to escape was finally catching up to me. What had I turned into? I was an emotional wreck. I was turning into a psychopath. I felt as if the world was against me. I can still remember the mental state I was in. I was truly losing my mind and it didn't help that I started to dip and dab with cocaine occasionally. It certainly didn't help that before going to bed I sniffed almost a gram of cocaine at Trina's house while bagging up for the drug spot I had taken away from Harry. One night, before one of our sex-capades, Trina persuaded me to use cocaine. She got naked and put the cocaine on her breast and had me sniff it off. Like I said previously, Trina had no hang ups when it came to sex, and she had a way of making me experience sexual odyssey every time we had sex. She was my sex tutor, and I was her willing pupil. I was eager to try anything that Trina suggested. I had no idea I was now entering uncharted land that was going to take me places I could never fathom. But nevertheless, Cassy sits up in the bed and hugs me and begin her lecture.

Starting off with "Unique this shit has got to stop! You're driving me insane! Not only do I fear for your life, but I'm starting to fear for mine as well. Unique I can't put up with much more of this!"

My alarm clock beeps. It's three thirty in the morning. I get out of my bed and lit a Newport. I stretched and sat back on the bed to put on my shoes. I walked over to my mother's room and go into the small safe and grab the twenty-five hundred dollars in crack cocaine. I had to go over to Putnam and Nostrand to re-up the spot that Dae was managing. As I went back into my room to kiss Cass, I noticed the light sensor in the back of the house was on which meant someone was in my backyard. I looked out the back window and notice movement in the bushes. I immediately grabbed my gun and begin to fire shots through the close window shattering glass everywhere. After maybe the fifth shot I noticed the bushes stopped moving. Cass is screaming and my mother is cursing me out mumbling a bunch of fuck words to me. All I remember her saying is, you stupid motherfucker! I run pass my mother, down the stairs to the back yard. I go outside with my gun in hand releasing more shots into the bushes. As I approached, I noticed that I shot a stray dog. I was extremely paranoid. The mixture of cocaine and all the beef that I had acquired had me stark raving crazy and straight paranoid. I mean I was bonkers. After realizing that I was totally off my rocker I turned around to look up at my bedroom window and noticed Cass staring down at me, shaking her head and still crying. I was embarrassed for allowing Cassy to see me uncomposed and in a partially induced state of thinking. The once cool, smooth, disciplined man was paranoid and irrational. That's not the person who I wanted Cassy to ever witness. Yet, she had witnessed this crazed man and I was embarrassed. I didn't bother to try to explain why I was carrying myself in such a deranged manner. I walked over to my car in the driveway, got inside and started the engine to warm the car up. I went back in the house to reload my gun before I drove over to the spot. When I got back to my car, I immediately opened the glove compartment and grabbed a baggie of cocaine. I kept them in the car and would occasionally give them away to people to encourage them to spend money at my establishment. But only this time it was me who was going to inhale this glossy powder up my nose. I opened the package of cocaine and took a sniff and rockets shot off in my head. I was immediately stuck staring into space in a daze. What have come of me? Did I secretly want to die? This wasn't me at all. I closed my eyes and leaned back in the seat. My mind started to race then I heard a voice. Up until today I still don't know yet if someone was talking to me, or a voice within me warning me to change my ways. The voice repeatedly kept saying to me, Unique you're going to die if you don't change! My whole body became numb from the chemicals I'd ingested. After a few minutes, the temporary high and rush began to take a sobering shock of what the fuck I had done. I begin to snap back to reality. I then slumped deeper into the seat, totally oblivious to the frantic stares of Cassy and my mother who were now standing outside of my car.

My mother's sailor mouth brought me back to the realization that I was slipping into darkness, meaning a world of trouble. Then I heard wailing police sirens. My mother yells, "you better leave now boy! Don't you hear those sirens!?" I put the car into gear and drove off. When I get to the spot, I knock on the door and hear the familiar voices of my crazy ass comrades. Dae and Truth always greeted me with genuine love you no longer see. After talking shit to the two of them through the door. Dae-Dae finally unlocks the door with Truth standing on the side behind the door waiting to play fight, but Dae gave me a head nod indicating that Truth was behind the door. I kicked the door smashing Truth behind the door busting his nose. Dae-Dae fell to the floor, hysterically laughing as Truth stood there looking like an angered psychopath with his nose bleeding. In all honesty I kind of wanted to hurt Powerful-Truth. (why?) I don't know. But maybe because I was upset with the fact that I was slipping. So, I was angry with myself for not being on my square the way I was conditioned to be. Then Dae looked in my eyes and said, "say word to the mother this nigga is coked the fuck up Truth!"

I walked pass Truth and Dae-Dae, headed toward the mini bar Harry left in his room. Me and Dae made sure the mini bar was stocked with all types of drinks.

Instinctively I poured me a screwdriver and tossed it down. I desperately needed to stay high. The reality of what I did was too fucking agonizing but, I knew deep in my heart and soul that no amount of drugs or alcohol was going to erase what Cassy and my mother had just witnessed. Which was a smooth ass nigga off his square, totally playing myself by using cocaine. Knowing the result of using drugs was me deteriorating into a nobody type of dude. A typical loser! For the most part regardless of how tough I was, I felt bad that I allowed myself to be enticed by Trina. Influenced to sniff cocaine and even worst, I let three of the most important people in my life see me weak and abnormally. In a weak position, which was totally out of my character. I couldn't allow that to happen again. Especially since I felt as though I had to be the savior of my mom, sister and girlfriend. Contrary to popular belief, although I had pimped women before, I have always secretly demonstrated the greatest devotion to females in one way or another. How couldn't I? I honored and respected my mother so much because as far as I can remember, she displayed a strength in herself that isn't commonly found in black women, and she passed it on to me. For a long time before I developed my own sense of integrity and principles, I lived by what my mother thought integrity was. And as sad at it is, my mother's perception was the morality of a pimp or a womanizer. Later in life due to the conditioning of my wife, I learned that women are one of the most important factors in this world. Because through her, I brought forth new life, my beautiful innocent children.

I felt abstract and removed from my manhood because I felt as though I had proven to be weak when I was taught to be strong. Somehow deep in my heart I just knew that I had disappointed, both my Mom and Cassy. After maybe five minutes Dae-Dae approached me with another shot of booze. This time it was a bloody Mary. Dae sat beside me and just watched me geek. I was clenching my jaw bones and frantically rocking my body back and forth. I was on the verge of a nervous break-down.

I was only in my teens and was already emotionally drained and totally beaten up by Mr. Streets. The streets had taken a toll on me. The guns, the drugs, the women and the responsibility of having to provide for myself, my mother and my sister was as symbolic to having the weight of the world on my shoulders. As Dae sat beside me, he slid his arm around me and said to me "been there bro." He pulled me close to him and said again, "Trust me, I've been there brother. It's going to be alright." This was his way of showing care and concern. He knew the burden I carried because he too was under the same pressure. Our lives were similar in so many aspects and that's why we were so close. We totally identified with each other's joy, pain, ups and downs. I wasn't exactly aware of what was happening, but I felt the power of Dae's concern.

After maybe a half an hour of just sitting on the couch, the euphoria mixed with the feeling of paranoia was starting to leave my body. I then stood up and asked Truth if he could go get me something to eat from the all-night Bodega because I was now hungrier than a runaway slave. Suddenly, I received a beep. The code on the screen of the pager revealed a code of numbers that Ray had given me. The instructions after such beep were to call Trina and she'd relay the message from Ray. I immediately called Trina and she said, I was to meet someone at 3pm at the Kingston lounge. Before Trina hung up the phone, she suggested that I come by her house for breakfast around 9am. I agreed, but really had no intention of going to see Trina because all she really wanted was to have sex. I then hung up the phone and told Dae-Dae to wake me up around 10am because I needed some rest. Dae threw a blanket over me, and I fell asleep right there on the couch. 9:30 that morning I was awakened by the C74 MOD 8am wake-up call. Yet I wasn't in C74. C74 was a building on Riker's Island that housed some of New York City craziest and wildest adolescents. Me and Dae served time on Rikers Island together and the correction officer that ran that housing unit name was C.O Thornton. Thornton would wake us up by saying "grab your socks and grab your cocks. On the chow you little motherfuckers!" Thornton was cool and as sad as it may seem Thornton was a role model to a lot of us.

He was at least six foot six and was muscular and strong. He was fair and firm. Believe it or not, a lot of us adolescents learned how to conduct ourselves as young adults and to carry ourselves as dignified human beings regardless of our then present situation.

But nevertheless, that's how Dae-Dae woke me up. Screaming "grab your socks and grab your cocks!" He also had an egg, cheese, and turkey bacon sandwich on toasted wheat bread and a cup of hot coffee. Before departing he spun around and said,

"you all alright nigga?"

Concerned about the way I had behaved the night before. He was serious for a moment then he started laughing. I said, "nigga what's so fucking funny?" He replied, nigga you better leave that shit alone!" I went into the bathroom to throw some cold water on my face. Then went into my pocket and pulled out my pack of Newport's and took one out and lit it, without brushing my teeth. I stood there staring into the mirror that hung above the sink and for the first time in my life, I admitted to myself that I didn't like what I saw. It wasn't that my physical appearance had changed because I wasn't that deeply involved with using drugs at that point. However, it was a feeling from within that I wasn't comfortable with. The feeling which a live wire nigga gets in his gut when he knows he is shortchanging himself and slipping off his square. Shit I was too smart for this stupid shit that I was doing especially since I knew better. I knew I had no business fucking with coke. I've seen first-hand the end results of what drugs did to people. My uncle Charles was addicted to shooting heroin and cocaine. He was once a handsome man with Muslim principle. Once he got involved with shooting drugs, he turned into a different kind of person. I mean in all honesty, he'd become extremely friendly and playful, but like everything in life there are pros and cons. Because when my uncle didn't have that shit, he would stick up anything. He would even steal from my grandparents so; I knew exactly what that monkey on your back could transform a human being into. Years later my uncle eventually died from HIV/Aids as a result of shooting heroin and cocaine. Somewhere deep inside of me, I knew better! I focused in on my inner strength and look back into the mirror and say to myself. "Nigga straighten up! Jack your pants! Lace your boots! Pop your collar and get back to what you're supposed to be doing! What you're not supposed to be doing is using this shit! I have people in my life who depend on me! Then suddenly, a song by McFadden & Whitehead popped in my head. The name of the song is "Ain't no stopping us now." I looked in the mirror and begin to smile while singing the words to the song. It went like this….

There's been so many things that's held me down but now it looks like things are finally coming around. I know we've got a long, long way to go and where we'll end up, I don't know. But we won't let nothing hold us back, we're putting ourselves together, we're polishing up our act, well. And if you've ever been held down before, I know you refused to be held down anymore!"

Out of nowhere, I hear Truth and Dae singing along from the other side of the bathroom door. I began to laugh while staring into the mirror. I stop singing and

Dae and Truth continue to sing the song. After they finished the song, I opened the door to exit the bathroom and get bum-rushed by my two comrades, pulling me to the floor punching and wrestling with me. My niggas yeah, my niggas.

Later that evening I appeared at the Kingston lounge. As soon as I entered, Trina immediately gave me a lecture on why I stood her up. Her exact words were "mother fucker I ain't one of those pissy-tail ass young girls. I told Trina I overslept, and she eventually forgave me. She said, Ray wanted to speak with me in the back.

When I get to the back of the lounge, Ray was standing by the juke box listening to some music, drinking a glass of Remy Martin. On this day in particular, Ray had on a navy-blue Captain's hat, a white linen short suit, and a pair of Gucci shoes, which was rather odd especially for Ray's age. But like always Ray was dapper, looking like brand-new money. As I approached Ray, he didn't waste any time informing me of my mother calling him. She told him about my behavior, and he should have a talk with me. I don't quite remember what explanation I gave him, but he lectured me and told me that even cars break down if you don't maintain good maintenance. He said that a person should take care of their bodies as if it was a foreign car. Even as to what type of oil and gas they put in it. Right there I knew he was indirectly telling me that he knew I only behaved the way I did due to using drugs. While Ray is lecturing me, Trina is sitting in one of the booths with her legs crossed eavesdropping on me and Ray's conversation. Ray looked over and spotted Trina listening. He yelled "bitch find some business! Can't you see that this is a confidential conversation!" Trina got up and walked to the door and stood outside in front of the lounge. She turned around to face me and Ray. Through the glass door I could see Trina stick her middle finger up at the two of us. Ray goes into his pocket and pulls out twenty-five cents and drop it into the jukebox and selects a song. The song that he selects is "Candy" by Cameo. Then he starts his confidential conversation. He immediately went into whisper mode.

After our conversation I went to the front of the lounge and knocked on the window seeking Trina's attention. Trina turned around super fucking pissed and I found it kind of cute and sexy. Trina came back into the lounge, and I grabbed her hand and hustled her away to the back entrance that led upstairs to the apartment Ray owned. She tried to resist but, she was faking it. I grabbed her, pulling her into me. I licked the side of her neck and placed her hand on my hard dick. "Don't act like that, we have some reacquainting to do." I whispered in her ear. Trina couldn't resist, right there in the hallway I had Trina faced against the wall, dress above her waist and beating that poo-nanny like a Mexican pinata until we both climaxed. I pulled my pants up and gave her a kiss on the cheek and left Trina standing there. I turned around and blew her a kiss and began to sing the words to
Cameo. "Trina is just like candy baby." Trina broke out laughing but not forgetting to ask whether I was spending the night with her or not. I told her that I would see her tonight.

After a night of hot sticky passionate sex with Trina, I arrived back to my mother's house around 10:30 in the morning. As soon as I walked into the house, Cassy was sitting at the kitchen table drinking a cup of herbal tea and reading the morning paper. I walked up to her and tried to place a kiss on her cheek. She quickly swayed back refusing my advance. "Oh, it's like that?" I asked, referring to her silent statement. "Exactly like that!" She said. I then mushed her in the face playfully and she jumped up to swing at me, trying to connect with my face. But I playfully grabbed her and spun her around and started playfully humping her like a dog in heat. She laughs and I whispered in her ear.

"Are you supposed to be upset with me? You know that you can't stay mad with big dick daddy." She responded with, "the only thing big about you is that big head on your shoulders little dick daddy!" "Now that wasn't nice now, was it?" I say. Then we both laugh hysterically. I make a sexual gesture motioning to the bathroom so that I could get me a taste of that Puerto Rican snatch, but she was not having it. I kept trying to make my move but the more I tried, the more she refused. It got to the point where I started to get upset and a bit aggressive. "Unique stop!" Cassy yelled. My mother appeared at the top of the stairs and said, "nigga leave that girl alone with your horny ass. You need to wash your before trying to get some pussy! As a matter of fact, bring your nasty ass up here, we need to have a talk!" I smacked Cass on her butt and went up to see what my mother wanted. Once I entered my mother's room she was sitting on the edge of her bed. She patted the bed, motioning me to sit beside her. Before I could even sit, she started with her lecture. Unique what the fuck do you really want out of life because as of lately you're really starting to frighten me and your girl. She then went on to say, I needed to find something to inspire and motivate me and that I needed to do something productive. The one thing she didn't do was discourage me from hustling, but she said, "baby everything in life runs its course. I need you to start thinking about taking some form of business or vocational trade so that you can get out of the game. She then went on to say, she could remember when boxing was something I loved unconditionally, and I should pursue my heartfelt dream of one day becoming a professional boxer with greater conviction. She said, if you put as much energy into boxing as I did with street life, she more that sure that I would become a professional boxer if I wanted to.

As my mom continued to lecture me, it turned into a guilt trip. It always ended up that way. She started blaming herself for the decisions I was making in life. I kind of felt sorry for my mother considering, she felt responsible for the way I was living my life. The bottom line was, regardless of what my mother thought, it was my ambition to become a gangster. And once a person has his or her mind made up to achieve something, it's extremely difficult to change their state of mind or perception about life. The reality was that deep down in my heart I knew I had to change my perception about life. But as far as I can fucking remember, I valued life based on the street life and what people thought Unique should be. Not by the true essence of who I was or what I really wanted. My value of life was totally linked to having a reputation and distributing an existing commodity, whether that commodity was dealing drugs or pimping women. I had already accepted my fate. I had already digested the pre-ordained notion that I would probably die by getting shot down in the streets like a bad guy in one of those old western movies. I had no problem with getting gunned down in a blaze of glory on some Clint Eastwood shit like in the movie; "The good the bad and the ugly, or even in the movie, "A fist full of dollars." Yeah, I was cool with that ending. Or a more updated movie such as "Set it off" which starred Jada Pinkett Smith, Vivica

A. Fox and the undeniable Queen Latifah. Set it off was a great movie with a heartfelt ending, no matter if you were recalcitrant toward scenario or not. After the conversation with my mother, I attempted to do some soul searching which only lasted for maybe three to four days. But without a doubt, the intriguing voices of the streets kept calling and like a fool in love I immediately went back to the love of my life. (The streets).

Preston Bradley said,

"I've never met a person, I don't care what his condition, in whom I could not see possibilities. I don't care how much a man may consider himself a failure, I believe in him, for he can change the thing that is wrong in his life anytime he is ready and prepared to do it. Whenever he develops the desire, he can take away from his life the thing that is defeating it. The capacity for reformation and change lies within."

Preston Bradley

CHAPTER TWENTY-THREE
GANGSTER GENTLEMAN

Dae looks at me, shakes his head and says, "Unique you're bugging! We have business to take care of, and you're sniffing that dumb shit before we handle business. I said, "nigga I'm only sniffing this shit to stay awake. We've been couped up in this van all day and night sitting on this bitch made ass nigga." Truth interjected; "shit then why haven't you touched the coffee Cass put in that thermal container for you?" "Because cocaine taste better motherfucker! Shit, don't be questioning me anyway?" I said. Truth laughs and says, "fuck it cocaine and coffee it is then." Dae looks at the two of us and says, "word to mother you two niggas are dickheads! Yall niggas better be focused because yall know this dude we coming for is packing! Furthermore, word on the streets is that he's dressed a couple of cats mothers in black. If you know what I mean." "Man fuck that nigga!" I shouted. When we grab him, you might as well stick a fork in his ass because his bitch ass is done!" Truth says, "yeah done son!" "Well both y'all niggas better get your fucking forks ready because this dude is pulling up right now into his driveway." Dae said, interrupting the laughter. "Listen, remember how we planned this shit because dude is strapped and supposed to be as equally dangerous as we are. When he gets out of the car and go to the back and retrieve his grocery bags, that's when we'll make our move. Again, remember how we planned it. There he goes now."

We rushed across the lawn as soon as he stuck his head in the back seat. He must've heard the rushing noise of our footsteps running in his direction. But when he looked up to see what the commotion was, it was too late. Two masked men were behind him with drawn pistols, daring him to make a move. He complied, as they usually do. But within seconds Truth slapped him upside his head with the 357. I can't front, I kind of dug homeboy's style. He responded to the slap upside his head with, "man is this about money, or am I fucking one of you chumps bitches?"

Behind my mask I smiled. I admired homeboy's cocky but smooth characteristic. I said to myself this dude is indeed a gangster. Then we rushed homeboy off to our awaiting van and threw him inside. I jumped in behind him. As soon as we all were inside the van, Dae mashed his foot on the accelerator. The customized van engine started whining as the tires dug into the ghetto black tar pavement as the van sped away. The nigga was as cool as a cucumber. After a moment of silence, I asked Truth, "yo, did you prep the spot nigga?" Trying to instill some fear into dude but, he remained silent except for an occasional sinister chuckle. Then out of nowhere he said, "okay Unique where are we going?" I'm like, oh shit! How does this cocksucker know who I am. I didn't respond. "Okay then, maybe mister Truth might know where we're going." Still nothing... Then he became as serious as cancer, talking in a shrill frightened voice. He said, "come on Unique what's happening? Look man I never meant to come down on Trina like that. I didn't find out until later she was your bitch. Man, I got your bitch bread Unique. Listen man, here's what I'll do, when my wife leaves for work tomorrow, I'll give you the keys to my house and yall niggas can go inside and retrieve the bread I owe Trina." "Yeah, nigga that definitely sounds like a plan to me. But you do know we are going to take something extra for our troubles?" "But of course, that's a small thing. Besides only a fool puts all his eggs in one basket." He said. I had to admire dude being cool as a cucumber was an understatement. I said, "well get prepared for this all-night slumber party." Again, homeboy responded with his sinister chuckle. Followed by the occasional statement, "its' all good, it's all good!"

Around ten in the morning I pulled up to dude's house and went in to retrieve my baby girl's cash and some work he had stashed in his floor model television/record player. He had it gutted out and used for a stash compartment. After retrieving the money and the work, I called to a corner payphone we occasionally used for making deals and situations such as this one. Dae-Dae answered the phone.

"Yo what's the word?" "Dae you can let him go!" "Oh yeah, okay." Dae said. "Why are you saying it like that?" I responded.

He says, "Unique this nigga is definitely a gangster gentleman. "I'm like, what brought you to that conclusion."

Dae said, "this dude is talking about, he's sorry about what took place with your girl. That he understands this was done in the name of business, and how would we like to go back to his crib and have a glass of wine to show that there's no hard feelings." I said "yeah, dude is definitely a bit too smooth, but I have the upmost respect for him. Anyway, just drop homey off by the Interborough Parkway and meet me back at my mom's house to divide up the extra bread. I don't need the money. I'm fucking the goose that lays the golden egg." "Yeah, we know that!" Dae said. And hung up the phone before I could even say something in return.

"What's up baby girl why did it take you so long to answer your phone?" "I was in the shower washing my ass if that's okay with you!" Trina responded. "Yeah, douche that pussy because the last time I hit that thing, it smelled like straight tuna." I said jokingly. "Nigga please!" Trina said. I was only bullshitting because Trina always smelled like a bed of roses. I inform that I had her money and that I was on my way over to her house but not before stopping by the Spanish restaurant to get food. When I finally reached Trina's building, I felt something strange in the midnight air but, I couldn't quite put it together. My street instincts mixed with common sense made me realize that I probably made a mistake by not pushing homeboys' wig back. I just realized I did something stupid. I snatched a nigga from in front of his crib, held him overnight at gun point, then robbed his crib of a couple thousand dollars and some heavy weight in cocaine. Deep in my heart I knew homeboy was going to retaliate. But anyway, I pulled into Trina's parking lot and pulled the car into Trina's reserved parking space. Before exiting the car, I gripped my 45 and grabbed the bag of food with my other hand. I kicked the door closed with my foot and walked across the

parking lot into the back entrance of the building. Once inside, I hit her on the intercom, and she buzzed me in. When I get upstairs to Trina's apartment, she had incense burning and wearing a red robe over her naked body. Her body was glistening with body oil shining like new money. I already knew what she had in store for me that night especially since she had a joint of Thai stick burning and a bottle of Pipers champagne on her piano. Trina wanted the African leather snake and damn if she wasn't going to get it. I watched in awe as she sashayed across her pearly white carpet to place the bag of food on the table. I can't deny Trina always found a way of keeping me in amazement. She had me wrapped around her finger, which was cool because within minutes, I knew I would have her wrapped around this dick. This woman knew exactly how to turn me on. I took off my shoes and put on a pair of slippers Trina kept by the entrance of her
door. I glided over to where she was and hugged her from behind. I grabbed her breast with one hand while grinding my hard penis against her ass. The

harder I pressed up against Trina, the more she threw it back. "Daddy is a little dirty." I whispered in her ear. I grabbed Trina's arm and lead her back to the bathtub. "How about washing daddy up?" I asked. Trina attempted to swat my hand away acting as if she didn't want it as bad as I did. I pulled her into me and pulled her into the bathroom. She still had her bath water in the tub. I pulled off robe and she stepped back into the tub with the bubbles completely covering her body. I immediately got undressed and got in the bathtub behind her. Once in the tub, I pulled her into me and began kissing her. Trina let out a sigh of ecstasy. I started kissing around the edges of Trina's lips. I took my time sucking on her juicy lips. She had what black people called soup coolers. I was into this kissing act because I became more aggressive. The kiss became deep and full of passion.

"Unique, you know how to drive a bitch crazy, don't you?" Trina moaned. I ran my fingers up and down Trina's arms. Then my hands found their way around and down to Trina's sexy petite ass. Firmly squeezing and gripping it. I then brought my hands around to the front of her love box and start massaging her clit. As I moved my finger in a quick motion, the stimulation was driving her stark raving crazy. Her legs began to quiver, splashing water out of the tub again. She began gyrating her hips to heighten the pleasure of my touch. I said, "yeah that's right baby, move with me. I slipped my fingers inside of her and started moving it almost as fast as the finger I had on her clit. It was a wrap! I took her all the way there as her body convulsed from the waist down. As her eyes rolled in the back of her head, I could see the immense pleasure she was experiencing. But I was far from done with her. I begin to suck on her breast, teasing her nipples with my tongue.

"Ooh baby my whole baby feels like it's on fire. Baby come on put out my fire." Trina said. I totally ignored her request. Instead. I said, "you like how daddy is making you feel huh?" She didn't answer she just continued to shake.

"Are you there yet baby?" I asked. "I've been there! Come on baby give it to me." I pulled Trina on top of me and inserted my manhood inside of her and she

began to ride me with her eyes closed. "Open your damn eyes, I want to look into your eyes." I said. She opened her eyes and rode me slow, up and down in a slow motion. She was a sexually expressive bitch and I loved it. "Unique I'm here baby! I'm about to come! Trina screamed. "Come on baby!" I responded.
I stood Trina up and entered her doggy style. Standing right there in the bathtub. I wasted no time. I didn't ease myself in either. I kind of rammed myself in forcefully not wasting any time. I was killing the pussy with every stroke. I was killing it so good, I yelled out, "bitch I'm going to need a lawyer in the morning because I'm murdering this thing!" Trina tried to laugh but the way I was stabbing at her, there was nothing funny. Then she started bucking back. She rotated her hips in a different motion. I grabbed her hips to better direct her moves. She says, "damn Unique, you're about to make me come." I then grabbed her in a neck choking position and went insane on that thing. I pulled myself halfway out and rammed myself back into her again and again until neither one of us could hold back any longer. "I'm about to come!" I yelled.

That day Trina realized that I was in love with the pussy because she turned around to face me and said, "nigga I got you pussy whipped." "Oh really? I'm not the one with the quivering legs. I can't front though you know how to put it on a nigga!" "And you know how to put it on a bitch!" Trina laughed. I got out of the tub and walked into the Trina's bedroom.

"Baby I need some time to recuperate so I'm going to lay across the bed and listen to the quiet storm but put the food in the microwave and bring me a plate. When Trina returned with both plates, I ate my food and fell asleep like a baby... In sweet Extasy!

CHAPTER TWENTY-FOUR
A HARD HEAD MAKES A SOFT ASS

(OLD SOUTHERN PROVERB)

I was awakened the next morning by a kiss on my lips, followed by a slap up against my head. "Are you hungry baby?" Trina asked. "Hell yeah, I'm hungry. But I don't have time for breakfast. I'll grab something to eat a later, but you can make me a cup of coffee while I wash my face and brush my teeth. I lit a Newport and walked into Trina's bathroom. When I returned, Trina had a hot cup of freshly brewed coffee. Trina knew how to cater to her man. Anyway, I got dressed and drank my cup of coffee. I called Trina over to sit next to me. "Yo Trina if you ever flip on me, you know I will kill your ass right." Trina laughed and said, "what happened mister hard rock I know you ain't catching feelings now are you?" "Anyway, you heard what I said." I kissed Trina and walked out the door. Once in the hallway, I stood by the elevator contemplating on the events of this past week that led up until this morning. I was starting to sense a change in myself. Was I falling for Trina? Was I becoming soft? Especially since I didn't off the nigga we kidnapped earlier in the week. I knew damn well that the only enemies who exist are the ones we allow to exist and that is exactly what I had done. My head was going in so many different directions. The conversation I previously had with my mom kept coming to mind. Damn I needed some time to get my thoughts together. I needed a vacation from all the drama and chaos. Maybe I'll persuade Trina to take me on a vacation. Shit, we both could use some down time from the everyday hustle and bustle. I had no idea I would get my vacation sooner than I expected. The opening of the elevator broke my thought pattern. I stepped on the elevator and pushed the button for the lobby. When the doors opened, I noticed a couple arguing. The female kept yelling, "so why won't you let me smell it then!?" Then she reiterated, "if you weren't out cheating then let me smell it!" I looked at homeboy and laughed. He responded with, "dude can you believe this shit?" I said, "trust me I've been where you are homie." I kept it moving, making my way to the parking lot. As I walked out of the building, the snow was beating me in my face. As I approached my car, a van that was parked next to me, doors opened. The occupants of the van jumped out and screamed. "Police, freeze and don't move!" They all had their guns drawn. Two more men came from around the car, which was parked on the left, with their guns drawn as well. One of the officers yelled, "yeah go for your fucking hammer and I will smoke your ass right here!" I looked up to Trina's terrace because Trina always made sure I made it to my car safely. Why, I don't know because she lived on the fourteenth floor and if something transpired, she wouldn't be of any assistance anyway. Trina was indeed looking off the terrace and had seen what went down. I heard her scream from the terrace, "don't worry I'll bail you out baby!" One of the officers cuffed me and threw me into the back of their panel van. But what was even crazier is that the driver of the van was the same nigga I had kidnapped a few days ago.

Damn these niggas caught me slipping. These niggas played the role of detectives, wearing badges and everything. Which was a great tactic because if they would have approached me any other way, I would have squeezed off a couple rounds into every last one of them. Homeboy who I kidnapped was sitting behind the steering wheel doing that same occasional sinister chuckle he did the night me and my boys grabbed him. He said, "Unique I'm going to show you how real snatch boys do it!" Snatch boys was a term used for cats that kidnapped as a profession and it was apparent that they had snatched a couple of people before. Especially since they came at me on some police shit showing badges, guns, cuffs and fake ass police radios. I sat on the floor of the van wondering what they were going to do to me. Were they contemplating murder? Or were these cats going to torture me then smoke me? I'm thinking, if they are going to kill me, I hope they make it fast and swift. Shit, I've been in the face of murder before. I'm not intimidated by the grim reaper. Shit, if it's going to happen then fuck it! I can't front or fake any jacks I was scared like a punk bitch watching a horror movie, but I wasn't about to reveal that. I wasn't afraid of so much being murdered. I was afraid of not being able to claim some position in my life. Meaning that there was so much that I hadn't done in life yet. And I'm not speaking from a productive conducive perspective. Shit, I still hadn't wreaked the havoc that I truly desired. Because I couldn't have wanted to live for anything positive although being positive wasn't my ambition, or was it? Could it be that the true essence of who I am is just a young man with no guidance or perception. And deep in my heart, body and soul, I was just acting out what I acknowledged as masculinity or the norm. Could that have been my truth? I didn't quite know, but one thing for sure and two things for certain, I wasn't ready to leave my present sphere or field of action. Not just yet. While all of this shit is going through my head, my thoughts were interrupted by a slap in the face. I was slapped in the face with a mac-11machine gun. After the slap, my head was cleared. I said to myself, damn this is it! I guess this will be my legacy. Dying at the hands of a foe because I failed to eliminate this cat when I was in position to do so. But I guess karma is a bitch. And just like mama said, a hard head makes a soft behind.

That's a true southern backwoods proverb. Then out of nowhere, someone approached me from behind and placed a pillowcase over my head and taped it around my neck. Then I felt a swift kick to my back, followed by a rain of punches to my head. Then someone hit me with a sharp object in the back of my head repeatedly. I tried to stand, but the attempt was interrupted by an instantaneous kick to my back. Suddenly out of nowhere I gained enough strength and ran headfirst into one of my abductors but was stopped by another rain of punches to my head. Then a sharp pain shot through my entire body starting from my neck to my feet. I dropped back to the floor of the panel van. After that, I couldn't feel any more pain. I could just feel the force of blows they were giving me. My complete body was limp and numb. I was now slipping in and out of consciousness. It's like every time I came to, I could hear the same sinister chuckle I heard the night I kidnapped homeboy. As soon as they realized I was conscious, they would begin their infliction on me once again. Followed by homeboy's sinister chuckle. Then one of my abductors said, "do you want me to off this nigga?" The cat with the sinister chuckle replied, "nah not right now. I'm enjoying this nigga's terror for now. Maybe we won't kill him and just kick his ass around a little more. Shit, I'm not sure what to do with him yet. The two guys lifted me off the floor of the panel van. While they held me, I was nailed in my face with some sort of blunt object, then they let me fall back to the floor. They all laughed as I squirmed on the floor in silence. I guess these niggas really enjoyed seeing me in a powerless position. Yeah, these motherfuckers were working me over pretty good in retaliation for kidnapping dude. Then suddenly, the van came to a stop and the side panel door opened. I was lifted to my feet and tossed out of the van into the freezing snow. They had beaten me so bad to the point where I was unconscious, then threw me into an abandoned lot. When I finally became conscious and opened my eyes, I realized that I still had the pillowcase over my head and my body was completely frozen and numb. Blood was dripping from my head, only to freeze against my skin. My hands were still cuffed behind my back and my fingers were completely numb. I tried to move my fingers but, they were unresponsive. That's the last thing I remembered. I later woke up in the hospital.

CHAPTER TWENTY-FIVE
PRAYERS & RELIGION

When I awoke, I felt intense pain in my body, mostly in my face. Damn, I had never felt anything like this before. Excruciating sharp pains shot through my entire body. I attempted to touch my face, then decided not to I was afraid, to do so, in fear of what I would learn. Then my mother, Trina and Cassy walked in the hospital room. I'm like oh my god, please not now! I just knew Cass and Trina were about to get into it. But Cassy had no idea who Trina was. My mother told her that Trina was an old friend of the family. Up until then, my mother had no idea I was in a relationship with Trina. I basically kept it on the down low. Trina and my mother hadn't seen each other in years, so this was a reunion amongst two rivals that date back to their teenage years. My mother came to my bedside and whispered in my ear. "What's up with this Trina shit?" She smiled at me and shook her head. Then suddenly, tears started pouring from her eyes.

"Boy where did I go wrong with you? Damn, I'm standing here looking at my baby boy in critical condition with all these tubes connected to his body." "Ma please not now. I really don't need to see you go on this guilt trip. You are giving yourself too much credit and blame. No one has the power to determine my fate. Because God has the power over all things!" My last statement set off a chain reaction because my mother got all Godly. "Nigga the only reason why you are alive is because of God Allah, Jesus or whatever you want to call the nigga!"

Here she goes, she didn't even recognize that she just called God a nigga. "Ma do you realize that you just called God a nigga? I asked.

"There you go, paying attention to all the wrong details. See it's not important what I called God. What's important is that I acknowledged He exist, and He is the omnipotent and without him, there would be no me and there would be no you!" "Oh my God ma please not now. And stop calling God's name in vain!"

I turned to my left and Cass is standing behind my mother with her face in the palm of her hand laughing. My mother turned around to Cassy and said, "what the fuck is so funny? And what famous Spanish bitch you think you are? Running around like you're Gloria Estefan and the sound machine. Or maybe you think you're that big head bitch Lisa Lisa. You think this shit is funny? Baby I know you believe in God because when my son has you up in his room slinging his little dick on you, all you do is call out God's name. We all laughed except for Trina. She walked out proclaiming to go to the hospital's cafeteria. Before she left, she turned to me and shot me some serious daggers. Boy oh boy, if looks could kill I would've died on the hospital cot.

When Trina left the room, my mother followed and said, "wait for me girl we've got some catching up to do." I know my mother did that intentionally to upset my goose who lays the golden egg.

When my mother and Trina went downstairs to the cafeteria, I found out from Cassy I had been in the hospital for two days and I had many visitors including the police. They had been there to question me but, I kept lapsing into oblivion, in and out of consciousness. She said after the second day I became aware of my surroundings. Although I couldn't see myself, I knew I was fucked up because I was in constant pain. Every time I moved a muscle, it was a reminder of the ass whipping I had received. Cass said, her and my mother were up for two days calling every precinct along with the FBI and other agencies in the surrounding boroughs trying to locate me. She said, finally my mom received a call from the 83rd precinct, located in the Bushwick section of Brooklyn. They told my mother that I was found nearly dead in an abandoned lot on Moffat St. and Irving Ave. But I was now in critical condition in Wycoff Hospital. They wouldn't give her any details or even what type of injuries I had sustained but, they needed her to come to the hospital to identify me. What happened was, they had taken the beeper they found on me and called back every number that tried to contact me. That was how Trina, my mother and Cass found out what was going on. After Cassy filled me in on what had taken place over the last two days, Trina and my mother returned to my bedside. My mother told Cass to take a walk with her to the gift shop so she could pay to have my hospital television turned on. As soon as she and my mother left the room, Trina went in. But to my surprise she was cool, calm and collective. She said, "so that's your little girlfriend huh? I'm not tripping, at least you have taste in women. I think she's cute. Does she like pussy?" "What the fuck are you talking about Trina?" I asked. "Boy you better get a clue that girl is bi-sexual." "Trina, you always got some other shit on your mind." "Okay, you don't have to believe me. But I know a bitch who appreciates the acquired taste of sweet pussy or enjoys having her pussy ate."

"Trina, I don't want to hear this dumb shit you're talking. What about asking if I'm okay or not." "Nigga I know what you're made of, and I know you're okay. I hope they didn't damage your dick because if they did, you better learn how to eat some pussy. And ask your girlfriend if she'll join us one night! I will suck that little bitch pussy until her head caves in." "Trina, listen I don't want to hear that bull dyker shit!"

Trina laughed but I honestly didn't find a bit of what she said funny! But I can't front, I visualized Cass and Trina together. In fact, it did sound like a great idea as far as I was concerned. Besides, I doubt if Cass would ever participate in such event.

Anyway, after a few weeks I began to heal. I no longer needed to be fed intravenously. My strength was starting to come back, and I began to feel stronger. I had been on bed rest for like three weeks. As I progressed, I was able to communicate with the doctors and nurses. One morning, the Nurse aides came in to give me a sponge bath. This Nurse was fat as hell but, she had a touch that was out of this world. For some reason, I found this fat nurse so sexy. She looked into my eyes and dipped her sponge into the wash pan and grabbed my manhood with one hand and washed me with the sponge with the other. After she got it all soapy, she intentionally rubbed it in a sensual manner. My manhood shot straight to attention, but it was painful because I had a catheter tube inserted into my penis. When I got erect, the pain was unbearable. The Nurse laughed and said, "I see that you are getting healthy again Mr. Battle and left the room. Later that afternoon when she came back to bring my lunch, she walked in laughing at me. She spoke in a West Indian accent.

"I can tell dat you one bad boy! I love the bad boys dem; but Mr. Battle you better watch how you move in dem streets dem; and better you seek some God in your life." She then spun around and left the room. Her last statement had me pondering on this whole God thing. Later that night I had a frightening dream. In the dream, I was standing in front of some counsel of some sort, and I was being reprimanded for rejecting faith and was given an ultimatum to either change my life or die in eternal fire. But the ironic part was when I awoke the next morning, I had two visitors. It was my Aunt Betty and my grandmother. Aunt Betty wasn't really my Aunt. She was an old friend of the family who dated Ray back when they were children growing up in the south. When Aunt Betty came to New York, she got involved with the Nation of Islam. Anyway, when I opened my eyes there was my grandmother holding her Holy Bible and

Aunt Betty held the illustration of the Holy Qur'an. Boy did they beat me in the head with religion. My grandmother kept screaming something about the blood of Jesus which I didn't pay much attention to because my grandmother was the epitome of a sinner. But Aunt Betty lived what she spoke. And every time she would come to family gatherings, she represented the Nation of Islam. She didn't smoke or drink and always spoke on some productive shit. So, if there was anybody I was going to listen to, it would've been Aunt Betty. I still remember today the Surah she read to me. It was Surah 11 the prophet HUD from the Qur'an. After what seemed like an eternity of a class on religion they left, and I immediately drifted off to sleep.

CHAPTER TWENTY-SIX

I LOVE YOU BUT I HATE YOU KING HEROIN

I was later wakened by Trina. Only this time, her visit lasted seconds because Trina came beefing about Cassy, I told her to leave. I was in too much pain to deal with her bullshit. At first, she refused to leave, but the presence of my uncle Charles and one of the Nurse aides standing in the doorway calmed her down and she eventually left. Trina left me lying there with a pulsating headache that complimented the pain I had already in my bones, and face. When they say the devil is busy, please believe it. I was in a lot of pain, but the Nurse's couldn't administer any more medication to me. That was the day I fell in love with Mrs. Heroin herself. After weeks of being pumped with antibiotics, painkillers, sleeping medications and shit. It had obviously caused me to become co-dependent of the drugs. "Nigga you look like you're hurting!" My uncle Charles said. I got something that will knock the pain off and knock you on your ass at the same time. But you are not ready for that type of ride. This here is some grown man shit. This ain't for no little niggas like you. Not only did I want to ease the pain, I also took what he said as a direct challenge to my manhood. Even though I was clueless as to what made a man, I still wasn't going to allow anyone, anybody or anything question or challenge my masculinity. So, I accepted the challenge head on. If there was anything I was willing to die for, or fight for, it was the prestigious title of being a man. In which most males never earn because for one, most men have no idea what manhood is in the first place. So, I say "nigga let me get that! What the fuck are you talking about. Nigga I been a man all my motherfucking life." My uncle chuckled and said, "you ain't lying boy. Shit I can't remember you ever being a child nigga. It's almost like you've been here before." "Man save all the bullshit and pass that shit." I say. And he passed it. Once he passed me the glassine bag, I stared at the bag in my hand for a second contemplating whether I should use this shit. I had already seen how it had cheated my uncle Charles out of a healthy productive life. Not to mention those I sold this same poison to when I was slinging this shit on Eldert Street in Bushwick for Mr. Big. My uncle Charles laughed and extended his arm reaching to grab the bag of heroin back from me stating, "nigga I told you that you ain't ready for this shit." But I pulled back refusing him access to the bag of heroin and blurted out at him, "nigga please!" I opened the bag by first unfolding it, then tearing the top of the bag off. Then I folded the top of the bag into the shape of an airplane, stuck the half that resemble the makeshift airplane into the bag. Then I took one big scoop and inhaled king heroin. The ironic part was that the name of the dope was named overdose which was symbolic to being named death. Was I fucked up in the head or was I psychologically fucked up in the head? Or was I again trying to define my warp perception of manhood? Again, no guidance and perception. Where's my Father? Nevertheless, I inhaled this poison like an avalanche moving in reverse up my nostril and immediately I wanted to vomit. My stomach went flipping, my mouth became extremely wet and watery. The taste of salt water filled my mouth. Then the taste was replaced with a more intense taste of salt water then I vomited all over the place. My eyelids became heavy. My whole body felt as if the weight of the world was now as light as a feather. I felt relaxed yet energized. I can't quite explain the feeling in which I felt but I know the heroin affected my penis as well. It became extremely hard, swollen and pulsating and I couldn't keep my hands off it. I just kept grabbing and squeezing it. Shit the way I grabbed it I was halfway semi masturbating I would suppose; I don't know. It was extra big, extra hard and it just felt so good touching myself. It was like I had a continuous climax or orgasm. The sensation I felt from using cocaine was nothing compared to the euphoria effect of the heroin. The heroin took me straight to heaven. For the first time in my life, I was at peace. Total ecstasy, ghetto paradise. I began to think, this is what heaven on earth must feel like. Then I nodded off into a sweet state of odyssey holding the half full bag of heroin in my hand. When I finally came out of my nod, Trina was sitting next to me in a chair eating Chinese food and watching tv. I asked Trina where did my uncle go? She said, he begged her for fifty dollars, she gave it to him, and he left. I guess he went to get his fix. It seemed as if hours had passed but, in all actuality, it was only minutes. After questioning Trina, I realized that I still held the bag of heroin clutched tightly in the palm of my hand. I had to hide it from Trina, so I pulled my hands up under the sheet on my bed and hid the bag of heroin in my socks. Within seconds Trina started her bullshit about Cassy again. As she went on complaining I got up out of my bed and went into the bathroom and shut the door behind me. I reached down in my sock and pulled out the half-filled bag of heroin and took a sniff. Once again, I experienced heaven. This time instead of squeezing and grabbing on my stiff phallus I planned to put it to use on Trina. For years I've heard all the old timers telling stories about giving females the "dope dick" which was a term used when you have sex for hours without climaxing. So, I looked into the mirror and smiled while saying to myself, "I'm going to give Trina the dope dick today!" Then I bust out laughing not really realizing how loud

I was laughing. I was so loud until Trina came into the bathroom inquiring what and why was I laughing all alone in the bathroom. I told her that I was laughing about how I'm about to beat her pussy up! I grabbed Trina, pulling her into me. She immediately followed suit by dropping to her knees and pulling my hospital gown up and placing my manhood in her mouth. Receiving double extasy because Trina was a savage when it came to performing oral sex. As Trina performed oral sex on me. I started singing Freddie Jackson's song "tasty love." Trina laughed, but never missing a beat while bobbing her head up and down like a bobble head on the dashboard of a fast v12 car. I aggressively pulled Trina off her knees and pushed her against the wall. Trina loved when I dominated her completely. She was like a lamb innocently anticipating my sexual slaughter, and slaughtering that box was something I intended on doing. I then kissed her on the bend of her neck while asking her who's pussy is this? She replied with, "Unique it's your pussy daddy." Then I started caressing the middle of her back seductively yet aggressively. I let my fingers drop lower squeezing her sweet supple ass. I then lifted her mini skirt and pulled her panties down, allowing them to drop and rest around her ankles. I put spit on my fingers to moisten her love hole before entering her. I entered Trina with extreme force. Her knees buckled as she shook uncontrollably. I started pacing myself like a skilled track star. Yet quickly speeding up the momentum with each stroke. She tried to buck back and the more she tried, the harder I thrust forward. Then I started to feel pain in my lower back from the ass whipping that put me in the hospital in the first place. So, I pulled out of Trina and sat on the toilet bowl, and she followed me. I grabbed her around her wrist and pulled her into me. My motion was self-explanatory she straddle me like a skilled cowgirl, while I just sat there in superfly Ron O'Neal mode, enjoying the pleasure I was receiving from this black ghetto bronco busting cowgirl. Me and Trina were so caught up in the rapture of our sex-capade that we didn't hear Cassy enter my hospital room. It wasn't until she punched Trina in the side of her jaw with a Mike Tyson hook that knocked Trina straight off my dick and on the floor. As Trina laid there in a daze trying to figure out what just crashed into her face, I sat there unable to move, stuck and ashamed. But before it was all said and done, Cassy jumped to the floor on Trina like a WWF wrestler. Straddling Trina, the very same way that Trina was straddling me seconds earlier. But she was throwing blows to Trina's face and head. Then Cassy became savagely brutal and grabbed Trina's hair, lifted her head off the bathroom floor and slammed it back down repeatedly. I stood there not knowing what to do. Moreover, I was totally stuck until Cass stood up and gave me a punch to my face, followed by a swift kick that landed me in the handicap bathtub. Damn, here I am lying in a handicap bathtub with my feet pointing upward looking like a football goal post or a homo thug caught with his legs in the air while his woman is giving him a rim job which was an inappropriate position no man should allow or get caught in. But there I was lying there more ashamed than physically hurt. I was kind of dazed because the back of my head crashed into the faucets in the tub. I quickly came out of the daze when I saw Trina stand up and make a dashing exit out of the hospital room.

She ran out my room like Jackie Joyner-Kersee. After Trina's dashes pass the Nurse's station, the West Indian Nurse came into my room to see what had transpired.

Upon entering my room, she yelled out, in her accent "bad boy what ta gwan in dis er room?" The Nurse stepped into the bathroom and saw me with my legs up in the air with my entire ass out. "What da blood clot is going on in here bad boy?" She asked again. I laid in the bathtub speechless while Cassy stood there enraged with tears rolling down her face. I felt like a loser. As I laid there staring at her, I could tell she was on the verge of snapping. She felt some type of way. I mean the kind that's deep and hot! I mean a straight dark wicked anger which probably surged through her entire body. I laid there with my ass out and my legs in the air contemplating whether I should move or not. Then she started moving closer to me with murder in her eyes. She moved like one of those psychotic bitches in one of those scary thrillers where the white chick loses her mind after being disapproved by her schoolmates for being socially different. The already crazy bitch just snapped like the chick did in the movie Carrie who vengefully start eliminating those who picked on her in the past. Yeah, that's the look she had in her eyes. And the way she was moving towards me was rather frightening. So, I tried to move as fast as possible, but Cass moved towards me even faster. Before I knew it, she pushed me back down into the tub. When I made an attempt to stand again, she knocked me straight back on my ass causing me to bump my head on the back part of the handicap railing in the tub. Then I said, "baby take it easy mama please. Listen to me it wasn't what it looked like." She says, "I'm so tired of your bullshit!" I attempt to interrupt to explain. "Listen, I say. Cassy screams, "no motherfucker you listen! For one, you're not in any position to be calling any motherfucking shots!" "Baby just wait one moment. Please let me explain Ma." I say again. "Listen faggot ass nigga before you start spitting what you call game. Coming up with all kinds of explanations to why you had this old bitch riding your dick! Save the bullshit apology or whatever you dog ass niggas want to call that lame shit. Let's just get one motherfucking thing clear nigga! I love you. I have always loved you and probably will always love your no-good ass! So, for once in your life if you ain't going to say some real shit to me Unique save it for the bitch who just hauled ass out of this damn hospital room. Then she spun around to leave and said, "oh by the way I came here to let you know I'm carrying your baby, but I'm not keeping it!" And she walked out. "Bad boy it looks like you done fuck up!" The nurse said. During me and Cassy's conversation I forgot that the nurse with the West Indian accent was standing outside of the bathroom door. But as soon as Cass exited, the nurse stepped into the bathroom with a smile on her face saying, "bad boy you betta try a fix dat." As she helped me out of the tub. This time I didn't even bother to respond. I just thought about the events that had just taken place. My goose that lays the golden eggs just got bum-rushed and cold coon-cocked knocked off her rocker and I just found out that my girlfriend is carrying my baby in which she's not

keeping. Damn!!!! I LOVE YOU BUT I HATE YOU KING HEROIN…

CHAPTER TWENTY-SEVEN

THE MESSAGE

Days had passed since the incident transpired and still, I hadn't heard from Cassy. Every time I called home my mother would pick up the phone saying boy you done fucked up because Cassy hasn't been here in days. My mother said, "Unique you really hurt that girl this time." I stood there with the phone in my hand speechless. I guess I was coming to the realization that I probably should had treated her better and considered her feelings. I should've acknowledged I had somebody who didn't care whether I was rich or poor. Someone who actually loved me for me. Damn, how could I'd be so stupid, selfish and so damn self-centered. Then my mother's voice comes back through the phone saying, "boy are you still there?" "Yes mommy!" I respond. She laughed and said, "I thought you hung up because you got quiet there for a minute. I said, "nah I'm here ma but, what are you laughing about?" She said, "nothing boy." I said, "nah tell me why you're laughing. She said, it's just funny how whenever your ass is in trouble or done fucked up, I'm not ma, I'm mommy." Then, she laughed and said, "but it's ok you'll always be mommy's little baby." I say, "whatever! Anyway, I'll call you later ma." Then hung up the phone. After hanging up, I thought about what my mother said about me using mommy instead of ma every time I was in trouble. She was correct. She was all I ever knew as a picture of strength, wisdom and endurance. So unconsciously I called my mother mommy in times when I felt weak, or needed strength, answers and remedies to problems and questions in which I sought resolution. But this time momma didn't have any remedies or answers nor any form of resolution for my broken, worried, and trouble heart. This time I had to fix this one all by myself. Or should I say, me and king heroin because after that unfortunate ordeal me and king heroin became better acquainted. The night before my release my mother and Trina came up to see me. Trina brought me a brand-new outfit to leave the hospital and my mother brought me a book. Inside of the book was an envelope but, she said that I shouldn't open the envelope until her and Trina left. She said to make sure I read a particular page in the book. The book that my mother brought up to me was my very own book. The name of the book was "Message to the Black Man" by Elijah Muhammad. Months earlier my mother had given me this book and suggested I read it. Only for me to toss it into the back seat of my car and there it stayed until she brought it to the hospital the night before my release. I accepted the book and placed it on the hospital night desk and gave my mother a kiss and asked her to excuse me while I talked to Trina in private. She kissed me again and backed up and threw a Bruce Lee kick in the air and started laughing. Come to find out, Cass told my mother how she Bruce Lee kicked me into the tub in the hospital bathroom. My mother exited the hospital room cracking up laughing. Once Trina and I were alone, she started kissing me all over my face telling me how much she missed me and loved me. Make no mistake at first, I was only using Trina as a sex mate until I found out how powerful she was in Ray and Danny's organization and discovered she was loaded and caked up with money. I was now actually growing feelings for Trina. But soon after the overwhelming display of affection she had for me; she went right back to that Cass shit. I stopped her in mid-sentence saying, "Trina please baby not now. We can talk about it when I get home." She says, "speaking of home, I guess I should inform you that I moved out of Brooklyn. I just brought a house out in Queens. Have you ever heard of Jamaica Estates?" She asked. I said, "No, I've never heard of Jamaica Estates. She went on to explain to that Jamaica Estate was a socialite community where Doctors, Lawyers and big-time music executives resided. She said, "as we speak Ray and brothers moving company are at the Co-op preparing the move to Queens so, I can't stay long baby. I'll be back here in the morning to pick you up." She gave me a kiss and walked away shaking and swinging her ass seductively knowing dam well that I was watching. Anyway, after my mother and Trina left, I immediately tore open the envelope. I knew exactly what was inside of it. It was an envelope with an address from the Island of Puerto Rico. My heart started beating a hundred beats a second because it was a letter from Cassy. On the other side of the envelope my mother had written on the envelope, baby please read pages 58 through 60 of the Book first. I tore open the envelope and inside of the envelope was a picture and a letter from Cass. I first grab the picture and kissed it as if it was her, I was kissing. Then I sat the picture down on the nightstand and begin to read the letter. The letter began,

Hello Unique, I'm not going to say much. However, I'm human and not like most humans I still allow my natural human facilities to take its natural course. Like for example, we can't help who we love once God puts that person into our lives. So, it's only natural that I'm still concerned about your stupid selfish ass. And the last time I saw you, you weren't in the best condition as far as health is concerned. However, you were healthy enough to get your dick up and hard. I want you to know that I'm not even upset with you for being a dog because I spoke with various male friends, and I also spoke to your stepfather about the situation. The way he broke it down to me, it made me understand how you guys think, and the fact that you were raised untraditional. Also, me and your mother have been talking over the phone and she surprised the hell out of me when she told me of her past. One would have never known that your mother was a female pimp at one point in her life. She explained to me that most men aren't into love, they're into conquest and each female who their able to conquer are like a medal of honor to them. And believe it or not she blames herself for your ways of thinking. She told me she taught you how to be callus when it came to dealing with the female gender because she didn't want any females taking advantage of you. She said that ever since she could remember you were naturally a sweetheart. In fact, that's what attracted me to you. You probably thought I was impressed with your bad boy gangster shit, but it wasn't that. Do you remember how we met? You met me in a vulnerable position, but instead of taking advantage of me, you comforted me and made sure that I got home safe. The next morning, I found out from Yvette that you pistol whipped Curtis for putting his hands on me and you didn't even know me. Then later that day you drove up on your motorcycle and yelled up to my mother's window screaming "aye you Spanish Puerto Rican girl with the long hair. Come to the window!" My mother came to my room and said girl I know that boy ain't calling up to my window like that for you. When I came downstairs to thank you, you grabbed my face, checking for scars and bruises. I thought it was so sweet, the way you cared for me, a stranger. Then you said, you'll be alright and jumped back on your motorcycle and drove off. Unique it was so sweet and caring; I fell in love with you that day. When I went back upstairs my mother asked me who you were and what was that about? When I explained to her, I didn't know you and that you were a friend of Yvette's not mine. She thought herself that what you had done was sweet. Later that night I went over to Yvette's house to inquire more about you and when she said, you managed her boyfriend's the weed spot, I made Yvette take me to the spot. I don't know whether it was the weed or not, but that night you reminded me of some type of political dictator. I was impressed by the way you managed the guys who worked at the spot. Especially since up until then, all the guys I dated depended on their mothers for income. Here it is you were out there doing what you had to do for yourself. I remember, we drove to your mom's house on your motor bike, and I held you around the waist. It felt so good just holding you and even though you were speeding and riding like a mad man I wasn't a bit afraid. I was confident that you knew what you were doing, and I felt safe. Damn Unique whatever happened? You have changed so much. Anyway, I miss you and I'm always thinking of you, but my mom and your mom think it's best for us to give each other space. They both concluded that absence makes the heart grow fonder and if it was meant to be, this space should pull us closer. Again, I miss you and I haven't made up my mind whether I'm keeping this baby.

    P.S. Love Always and forever,

        Cassy

I was truly touched and amazed by Cassy's words. I sat the letter down, picked up the picture and stared at it for a couple of minutes. Then I grabbed the book my mother brought to me and walked to the bathroom and read pages 58 through 60 of "A message to the Black Man" by Elijah Muhammad. Pages 58 through 60 were basically speaking of how a man should always treasure and protect his woman. He said, a female is a man's field to produce his nation and if he doesn't keep the enemy out of his field, he won't bring forth a good nation. He said, a farmer will go into his field and look for shit that will possibly destroy his crops but will kill whatever dangers his crops. Elijah Muhammad said, we should protect and nurture our women the very same way that we protect and nurture our crops. The point my mother was trying to make was that a crop is only as good as you nurture it, and a woman should be treated the same way. Because it is through her that humanity is created. I said to myself, yeah ma I get the picture. I went back to my hospital bed and turned the television on. Not really watching it, just pondering on my life and what I was going to make of it. I had to laugh to myself, thinking about my much-needed vacation. I didn't expect for it to be in a damn hospital. Then I dozed off for maybe four hours. While asleep I had a dream about me and Cassy. I can't quite remember everything in the dream but one thing I remembered was Cassy pushed me off a cliff and before I hit the ground, I woke up sweating with my heart beating fast as if it was going to jump out of my chest. I got out of the bed and went into the bathroom and put cold water on my face. I returned and pulled out a pen and paper to drop a few lines on Cassy. The letter begun like this.

Greetings, lady Sunshine,

I received your letter today and I must admit, you brought sunshine to my cloudy day. I was worried about your wellbeing, considering you were MIA (missing in action). Anyway, I hope that all is well with you out there in your native land. As for me, I'm maintaining and getting stronger by the day. But nevertheless, I don't know how to start this letter, but I guess I should start by being extremely apologetic for my polygamous behavior. I won't say it was a mistake because I was totally conscious of what I did and the reality is, had you not caught me I would still be doing the same shit. However, I think everything happens for a reason. It took me to do something stupid and lose you before I realized your value. I now recognize I had someone who cared for me with no strings attached. Royce told me years ago that boys make mistakes and men make decisions. At this point I don't know whether I am a man or still a boy tying to be a man. I think all my life I was incorrectly taught how a man should perform. I also think it has a lot to do with me being raised by a women and warped thinking criminals in the streets. Now I realize my ideal perception of what a man is, was totally wrong. Now that I'm a bit older, the only successful men I'd ever seen in the hood were pimps, drug dealers and stick-up kids and for the most part, most of them cats were womanizers. I guess what I'm basically trying to say is, I've made a lot of mistakes and I'm sorry. I was thinking like a little boy, or maybe I wasn't thinking at all. I really don't know. I'm still trying to figure out the actual etiquette of a man in the first place. In all honesty, I don't like how I was taught to treat women. Anyone who knows me, know I'm really a meek individual. Well not quite meek, but I believe I'm humble by nature at least when it comes to dealing with you, my mother and the females in my family. Basically, I feel as though I was conditioned by my mother to stomp down on a woman.

But when I brought you home my mother's ideologies about how I should handle and treat a woman changed

drastically. Speaking of my mom, she must really love and trust you because up until you wrote me the letter, I had no idea my mother was once a madam. I mean I knew she was type pimp-ish and aggressive, but into the white slavery profession, nah I didn't know. What else do you know about my mother that I don't know? Anyway, the woman never seems to amaze me. Her revealing those things to you should give you an idea of the principle in which I compellingly inherited. Anyway, again what I'm saying is I'm sorry and I'm begging you to forgive me and please don't kill my seed!! Stay sweet and come home.
Unique

Smooth-n-tuff

Elegant-n-ruff

CHAPTER TWENTY-EIGHT

MAKE MY FUNK THE P'FUNK

Diamond in the back sunroof top, nigga back on the scene with the gangster lean and leaning I was. Two bags of P'Funk for breakfast will usually put you on the lean first thing in the morning. Especially a special brand called "good year." Good year was the name of the most potent heroin around 1986-87 and I had to have it. During my stay in the hospital, I acquired a taste for heroin. After the doctors were no longer able to dispense pain medication to me, I started using heroin. Which was equivalent to the pain medicine I received, but heroin was much better. So, me and king heroin became the best of friends.

Me and my boys were packed in a car riding dirty with a shit load of automatic weapons. We were on our way to my adversary to get pay back for kidnapping and putting me in the hospital. Me Dae-Dae, Truth and Righteous were up early in the morning with the intent of causing somebody's family grief, sorrow and pain. This time the plan was totally different, it wasn't about money. I wanted him for a specific reason. This time I plan to torture him for a while. Causing him extreme pain, while he begged for his life. And if what I sought was denied, I was going to inflict more pain. Man, if we would've gotten pulled over by the cops, we would have been in a world of trouble because we all had two guns a piece on each of us. Here I was riding dirty, high off more than weed with my eyes blood shot red. Smoking my favorite Thai stick phat head joint with two bags of heroin already in my blood stream. If the police would have pulled us over, only God knows what may had transpired. We could have gotten ourselves killed by the police or things could had gone in a whole different direction. And considering we were high; we weren't in our right state of mind. No telling what one of us may have done. I think we were at the point in our lives where we were capable of banging out with the police on some Larry Davis shit! Thank God it didn't happen. Anyway, as we got closer to our destination, we began prepping ourselves for the abduction. We slowly crept down home boys block, driving around maybe five miles an hour. As we approached, I noticed the house had a sold sign posted on its lawn. Then I noticed there weren't any curtains in the window. I told Dae-Dae to pull over. We got out of the car and walked up to the house to look through the windows of the empty house. Homeboy packed up his shit and moved his family. "Yo, say word to mother this nigga got ghost. Dae-Dae said. "Word to mother. The nigga can run but he can't hide!" I responded.

Later that evening I was to meet Trina at her new house in Jamaica Estate. Man, I thought Trina's crib was fly in Brooklyn. Her new residence in Jamaica Estates was astonishing. Behind a tall white iron electric gate, there was a circular driveway with a water fountain which sat directly in the middle of the driveway. Trina's Mercedes Benz sat next to her Jaguar. Her house was equivalent to the homes you see on those shows Cribs, or the Lifestyle of the rich and the famous. When I saw Trina's crib for the first time, I realized she had more money than I expected. In those few years I watched Trina go from a bitch who ran a bar for Ray and Danny, into a smalltime drug dealer businesswoman with a two-bedroom Co-op in Brooklyn, into a self-made millionaire bitch who laid down some serious bread for a ten thousand square foot mini mansion in Jamaica Estates. I still remember the day I stepped foot into the fifteen bedrooms, nine-and-a-half-bathroom mansion. It was the day I was released from the hospital. Trina picked me up in her brand-new Jaguar and we went straight to her crib. I felt like God sitting in a classy ass car being driven by a classy ass bitch. On our way to Trina's house, she gave me a lecture. Then she kind of got cocky. I can't really identify how I should had perceived her attitude but, it was abnormal. Coming from her at least. But what she said was surprising because she came off as being arrogant. She started the conversation with "Unique now is the time baby. You've been with me since you were barely able to pee straight. I didn't build this shit by myself. You put a lot of work in for me in the streets and I want you to know that I appreciate… She then paused for a second. Then the words rolled off her tongue and she said "and I love you. There it is Unique. Yeah, I love you Unique. I achieved all I have based on your hard work, blood, sweat and tears.

I said, "But shit you supplied the work." "Baby and you planted the seeds and so it's only right I let you taste the fruits of your labor. You have contributed a lot of energy in helping me build an empire." Trina was right. I helped her build, so yes it was rightfully part of my empire. At least that's what I thought deep down in my heart, but I was unaware that Trina had secretly built a white slavery empire in which she had learned from the best, my mom. That's where the bulk of Trina's money came in.

Trina was a madam and a pussy peddler.

Even twenty odd years later I can still remember that day like it was yesterday. As I said previously, Trina exposed me to a whole different lifestyle. Anyway, when I reached Trina's later that evening there were a few cars in her driveway. Which was strange, considering that the type of business she was involved in was built on bloody money. When you generate money from some form of ill means, you may want to move under the radar. But this was different, Trina was having a small get together for her business venture which was the sex trade. The cars in the driveway were potential clients. She was letting them view her new product which were exotic women she had imported from overseas. When I stepped inside of Trina's house, I was amazed at all the barely naked women who were walking around the house. At first, I thought I was dreaming, or had died and gone to heaven (pussy heaven) that is. There was one female who caught my attention. She was from Saudi Arabia, and I was immediately struck by her beauty. She was an Arabian princess. I couldn't keep my eyes off her and Trina noticed. She said "Unique, don't let your dick get you into some bullshit you little horny bastard!" She yelled in a sexy yet assertive voice. I said, "baby please, I ain't thinking about that chick, which was a lie. I was totally inquisitive about this female, not so much because she was beautiful, but because she was so young. I thought to myself, how did this young innocent girl get involved with this type of shit. I was told that she came to the United States under the assumption she was going to pursue a modeling career. Only to later find out she would become a slave in the sex trade. The sad part was that her parents were involved with the whole manipulation process. They helped deceive and trick her into believing she was on her way to becoming a super model. Trina sat me down and filled me in on this young girl's past and history. Trina said, she had a twin sister who couldn't stomach the game and ultimately started using heroin to self-medicate. The reality of what she was doing was too much for her to deal with and eventually she died of an overdose. Trina said, she believed the Arabian princess was dipping and dabbing with heroin as well because the bitch always seemed to be tired or sleepy. After Trina told me homegirl's story, I went upstairs and laid across the bed thinking what life must've been like outside of the United States. Shit had to be extremely hard elsewhere because I couldn't imagine my mother selling my little sister into the sex trade. While laying across Trina's bed pondering, I eventually fell asleep thinking about the young female from Saudi Arabia.

As I lay in the bed dazed and half asleep. The Arabian princess had crept into Trina's room and begin to undress me. As I lay there motionless, she took off all my clothes and climbed into bed with me. Straddling me as she placed kisses on my bare chest and neck. Her lips were so soft and tender. I slid my hand around her soft caramel ass and started caressing it. I grabbed the back of her neck and pulled it forward placing a kiss on her lips then she then grabbed my manhood and stuck it inside of her. As I entered, she let out a moan. I could feel her juices oozing from her love box as she made my manhood so slippery and wet. She began to grind on my dick faster and harder, then I busted. I couldn't hold back any longer. Then I awoke from the dream to see that it was Trina who had undressed me and took her some dick while I slept and dreamt of the Arabian princess. I looked at Trina and smiled. I guess Trina thought I was smiling because she snuck some dick while I was asleep because she said, "I see you're smiling huh baby. I must have put it on you." "Yeah, boo don't you always." I said. I turned over and fell back to sleep in search of my Arabian princess.

First thing that next morning I was awakened by the sound of someone knocking on Trina's bedroom door. I didn't respond to the knock, but then there were three more knocks followed by a sweet foreign saying, "Unique I'm coming in." I immediately tried to position myself in a sexy posture. Exposing my bare chest in hopes of enticing the person with the sweet voice on the other side of the door. I blurted out "the door is open. Come in and don't let it slam behind you." She walked in and just like I anticipated, it was indeed Saudi. My Arabian princess was carrying a breakfast tray, which held a beautiful assortment of colorful food. Damn, Trina really done stepped her game up a trillion. On the breakfast serving tray there was vitamin A, vitamin C, vitamin D, fiber and protein. A complete healthy breakfast. Orange juice, toast, eggs, sausage and a cup of hot coffee. But the hottest shit that came in Trina's room wasn't on the breakfast tray, she was carrying the breakfast tray. There she stood in a short night gown. Her legs were so beautiful. Her breast stood erect looking succulent and delectable like a navel orange straight from Florida. I sat up in the bed and she handed me the breakfast tray. She said, Trina had to go to a business meeting of some sort in Manhattan, but she left instruction for her to prepare breakfast for me. When she gave me the tray, I grabbed her wrist and told her to come have a seat on the bed, but she refused. Then I tapped the bed gesturing to the empty side of the bed. I explained to her that I wasn't going to try anything. It was just that Trina told me so much about her and I just wanted to get to know her. "Trina doesn't think that would be such a great idea. In fact, Trina told all of us girls last night that we should stay clear of you but especially me." I chuckled and said, "Is that right? So, she said especially you huh? I wonder why that is?" "Trina said she saw the look in your eyes. I think it may be the very same look you have in your eyes right now." "Is it that noticeable? I asked. "Well yes, and I'm rather uncomfortable with this whole scene. I don't like this unique." Saudi replied. "You don't like what? I asked. Not once did I say anything indicating that I was attracted to you." She said, no not verbally, but the look in your eyes tells me a whole different story." "Is that so." I said, taking her hand and pulling her closer to sit down on Trina's firm king size bed. This time she complied. I bent forward and whispered in her ear. "I respect that you respect yourself and Trina, but I think what you are experiencing is called wishful thinking. But it's okay, I understand." She stood up and asked me if I needed anything else? I said no, and she exited the room. When she left the room, I let out a chuckle, laughing to myself because for one I acknowledged two things. The first thing I noticed was how nervous Saudi was in my presence and secondly, she was also attracted to me. I found her bashfulness kind of cute and funny at the same time. Anyway, after I ate my breakfast, I got out of the bed and dug into Trina's album collection and put on some sweet soothing Sade and went into the bathroom to take a shower. I washed my ass while listening to Sade sing "is it a crime" and naturally started singing along with the music.

CHAPTER TWENTY-NINE

BLACK WOMEN, YOU ARE PRICELESS

I arrive at my mother's house to find she was having a cookout. As I walked into the backyard, she was fixing herself a plate of barbeque chicken, potato salad and collard greens. When she turned around and noticed me, she sat the plate down and ran across the backyard to give me a hug. If you didn't know any better, you would've thought my mother was my woman. Which isn't uncommon in the black community. Usually, the women's male offspring must reciprocate for the short comings of her male counter- part. Especially in urban single parent households and it was exactly the case with me and my mother. However, this just made my love for my mother stronger and uncompromisable and she felt the same about me. I think it is safe to take the liberty to say that I was my mother's favorite male offspring. At least back then I was. But being her favorite entailed a plethora of problems and responsibilities which were equivalent to carrying the weight of the world, so the world I carried. Because I didn't want to let my mom down, I strived to take up my father's slack. Trying to phantom my very own course to manhood without having any idea where I was headed. I think part of the problem comes from us, as men not acknowledging our Queens for who and what they truly are. In all honesty, we must respect and honor the black women, for she is the mother of civilization. Once upon a time I didn't have a proper love and respect or an appreciation for women, other than my immediate family. I didn't grow an appreciation for a woman until I met my wife. I tried to fight and hold back my love for her out of fear she would get to know the sweet loving Unique I really was, but her ways and actions commanded respect. Not demanded but commanded. Before her, I couldn't care less about a woman and a million men like me have felt or feel the same. The way we treat or have treated women is seen every day and reflected in how she carries herself. A lot of women are promiscuous because we degrade them and make them feel as though they are only objects of our desires. Back in the 60's there were so many black kids born out of wedlock. In 1965, 24 percent of black infants were born to single mothers. I was one of those children who were born out of wedlock and practically raised by a single mother. As time proceeds the relationship between male and female is getting crazy. The word pregnant means full of meaning or significance. And the way to get pregnant is through sex so, if a male and female aren't ready to be a part of parenthood, then they should abstain from the use of sex or take precaution when sex is just a recreational thing. I'm not going to place the full blame on the male gender. Although women are allowing themselves to be used, allowing themselves to be disrespected and degraded. Allowing men to use them as sex objects. Bottom line male and female should stop having sex for recreational purpose. When a man leaves a woman to fend for herself and her offspring, it can breed some serious hostilities in the child and in the women. Anyway, my mother depended on me in so many ways and I refuse to not give her whatever it was she desired. Whether it was just paying a bill, buying her a used car, buying food for the house, or just giving her money. My mother depended on me. She would always say to friends and our family, "here comes the man of the house. Or I don't need no nigga my youngest boy is my man!" At the cook-out, I noticed my mom had been drinking. She was tipsy because she was starting trouble with her boyfriend Jefferey. (Pep) was his nick name. Pep was a stick-up kid/creep thief/tilt topper. He was deep into the streets. Anyway, Pep was in and out of my mother's life because he was constantly in and out of jail. Me and Pep eventually became close, not so much as a father figure but as a man who would go out of his way to protect me, my mother and all her kids for the most part. Pep was also a heroin addict. When I first met Pep, he was wearing a pony skin jacket, a pair of suede shoes with fake diamonds in them, a pair of sharkskin pants, with a beaver hat. He was fly as fuck. In fact, Pep taught me how to dress. Pep brought me my first pair of playboy shoes, my first mock neck, and my first pair of sharkskin pants. When I started hustling, Pep took me to his personal tailor on Broadway in Bushwick. The tailor shop owner name was Moons. All the hustlers went there to get their customized suits made. Anybody who was somebody went to Moons. All the fly cats went to Moon's. Pimps, drug dealers, con men, hoes, tilt toppers, stick up kids, butch kids, snatch boys, extortionist, dope fiends, the niggas who snatched money bags in midtown, three card molly cuts, boosters. I mean if you were in the game and living the lifestyle, Moon's tailor-made suits was a must. It was more-so a status symbol. Nevertheless, on this day at the cookout, my mother was talking plenty shit to Pep. And as dangerous as Pep was, he never put his hands on my mother. I mean, at least not in front of me. Anyway, after seeing how upset my mother had made Pep, I called him upstairs to my room and threw him a couple of gags of heroin. Not that he didn't have any money, it was just on the strength because Pep was a go-getter and always kept a few dollars in his pocket. Anyway, Pep told me that every time I came around my mother, she would start her bullshit comparing him to me. I totally understood how being compared to a woman's son could make any man feel, but I knew what it was all about. Pep was basically a good dude when it came to providing for my mom. She was just trying to impress me, or should I say she was trying to tell me how appreciative she was for all the sacrifices I made for her and my little sister. Pep wasn't a bad dude. If he could've left the heroin alone, no telling what he could've achieved. Anyway, I told Pep about a lick he could make, but I wanted a percentage out of it. Pep agreed to giving me a percent of the take. The job was a little under one hundred and thirty thousand dollars, but I didn't entail any real danger because it was basically an inside job. One night I was partying with a couple of females who I met at this club called Union Square. In fact, it was the grand opening night of the club. Hip hoppers came from everywhere, Harlem, Brooklyn, Queens, Bronx, Long Island, and Staten Island. If I'm not mistaken, that's the night LL Cool J got stuck up for his jewelry. Don't quite quote me on that, but outside of the club was where everybody gathered showing off their outfits and jewelry. Men in search of fine ass females with slick ass outfits, bamboo earrings and done up hair dos. And females looking for fly guys rocking cable chains, four finger rings, fresh haircuts and fly ass outfits. On this night I was wearing a pair of Stan Smith Green and white Adidas sneakers, some white shorts, and a green and white Benetton shirt. I had two gold teeth in my mouth and rocking a rope chain with a gold cross around my neck. That night I didn't go to the club with my boys. I went there with a chick I knew from Bushwick name Violet. Me and Violet left Brooklyn together, but we were to meet her girlfriends at Fourteenth St. and Union Square. When we reached fourteenth and Union square, Violet had at least seven females waiting on her. Man, Violet's homegirls were fresh to death. I mean I'm talking about some of the fly-est, boosting chicks ever. These broads were rocking name brand shit the average hood chick never even heard of. in all honestly if it wasn't for me fucking around with Trina and seeing some of the shit that she used to wear, I probably wouldn't have had the slightest idea what these chic's were wearing. The only brand that probably was recognizable was their Gucci sneakers. In fact, that was the name of the crew the "Gucci girls." Anyway, when we reached the club, some shit had already jumped off and as a result of that the club owner or promoter shut down the party. But everybody that came to the club didn't leave. They hung around in front of the club for a while just kicking the breeze, then eventually ended up hitting the Latin

Quarters nightclub. All that night me and Violet's friends got pretty acquainted. That night I found out from one her friends that Violet kind of liked me and up until then I had the slightest idea. I wish I had paid closer attention because Violet was cool people. Her homegirl Momo told me that Violet was big on me, and she thought that we would be good for each other. I explained to Momo that she may in fact be correct, but I don't fuck around with chicks who niggas I know. I told her that I had always been a man of morals and although I don't owe her man any loyalty, I just felt that men shouldn't deal with females until they closed certain doors. Momo stood in amazement at the conversation that we held but couldn't believe that I was a man's man. A man of principles, integrity and that I was proscribing to polygamist relationships. The reality was that I was already involved with multiple relationships and my plate was already full. Also, I respected Violet too much just to play mind games with her. She

deserved more than that. However, I had plans for Ms. Mo. Momo became rather cool to the extent as where we exchanged phone numbers and all. For a couple of months, Mo and I maintained a big brother, little sister relationship. Mostly over the phone because Momo was from Harlem, and I was from Brooklyn. Mo would occasionally come to Brooklyn and hang out with me while I was in the streets doing dirt. I would always introduce Mo as my little sister, and I noticed that she started catching feelings about the title that I placed on her. Momo truly dug me, and I dug her to the extent as where I wanted to sex her, nothing more nothing less. I just thought that she was sexy and easy to talk to. Plus, the fact that she was tearing Fifth Ave. up on some boosting shit was a plus. But I didn't really want to be involved in a relationship. At that point I still had a chick MIA in her native land of Puerto Rico that I intended to get back with. However, one night while visiting my mom's house, my beeper goes off. The code on the beeper is 212-911 which meant that it was an emergency in Manhattan. I'm puzzled now, because Trina has now extended her business to Manhattan dealing with white corporate executives. Then I had Mo out there living in the Polo grounds. My first instincts were to called Trina to see if my golden goose was safe. I called Trina to get cursed the fuck out. I called Trina and asked. "Hey baby you beeped me. And all hell broke out! She said, "mother fucker hell no I didn't beep your ass! It must be one of them young ass pissy-tail bitches! And why haven't you called me all day? Anyway, I didn't want to get into a long out conversation with Trina, so I told her that I was on my way over to her now. Fronting like I didn't like the way that she spoke to me over the phone and hung up. As soon as I hung up, I called Mo. She informed me that her boyfriend had just found my beeper number and he slapped her up thinking that we were fucking. She said that he slapped her around and snatched her earrings out of her ears, snatched of her chains from around her neck, spun her around and kicked her all up in her ass in front of her crew. I immediately asked her what did she expect for me to do? "Nothing, Unique but can I come to Brooklyn to see you?" Mo asked. I paused for a moment, then she said; "Unique I'm coming! Where are you?" She asked. "Mo I'm busy!" I say. I didn't want any parts of what Mo had going on. I had other things to worry about. "See, all of you nigga's ain't shit! I really thought if nobody else, I could depend on you! Unique I just don't want to be up here in Harlem tonight. I need to be around somebody that I can trust." I said, "Momo I'm at 510 Layfette street. I'll be here waiting for you." And I hung up the phone. When Mo arrived, you could tell that she had been crying her eyes out. Momo was a jet black, she had shiny beautiful black skin that was total y smooth and flawless. Yet, her face was now stained with white streaks from all the crying she had done. When she got out of the cab she practically ran into my arms and I put my arms around her, I felt her entire body go from being tensed to relaxed. That's when I leaned back yet still embracing her. When I looked into her face, I saw that she was an emotional wreck. I grabbed her hand and led her inside of my mother's house and sat her down on the couch in the living room. I then bent down and took off her shoes and told her to relax and that I would be right back. I went into the bathroom to get a wet face cloth and returned to the living room. I walked over to Mo and sat beside her and begun wiping her face. All the while, she's looking into my eyes like a sad puppy. When I noticed the look in her eyes, I smiled, and she began to laugh. It made me feel good that I was able to change her emotional state. She went from sad to happy. It felt good to know that my care and concern was appreciated and recognized. As I attempted to stand up Mo grabbed a handful of my cock, squeezing it tightly in her hand. As I fronted like I was trying to pull away, she gripped it tighter pulling me closer to her. Then she un-zipped my pants and bingo! Pop goes the weasel until the weasel went pop. I mean pop pop pop pop! Then I heard my mom coming down the stairs from her bedroom. When she reached the living room wearing that once fly sexy house coat me and Mo looked at each other and laughed. My mother came down the stairs in that old ass busted house coat/robe. My mother walked over to us and said, "hey stranger how my baby doing and who is this pretty little lady?" I introduced my mom to Mo, and then she went into the kitchen to get nothing at all. Yet, she pretended as though she came downstairs for something. I know dam well she probably seen when Mo pulled up in the taxicab and ran into my arms in front of her house. My mom knew how I was giving it up. She probably attempted to come down the stairs sooner but caught Mo doing her thing with my ding-aling. I thought it was ironic that as soon as Mo made the weasel go pop, my mother pop up. Anyway, she was basically being nosey! I kind of think she dug when I brought a young beautiful female home. My mother left the kitchen and went back upstairs to her bedroom empty handed. I grabbed Mo by the hand and told her to follow me upstairs to my bedroom. When she entered my room, she was amazed how organized it was and that it was painted pink. If you didn't know any better, you would had thought that I was a fucking homosexual or some sort with all of those teddy bears and stuffed animals and shit. I explained to Mo that I barely stayed at my mom's crib and that my mom and my actual girl was rather close, but I haven't heard from my girl physically in a few months only through letters but, my girl lived there. I told Mo that I was very much still in love with her, and that I planned on fixing shit when she got back from Puerto Rico. Me and Momo laid in my bed for hours sharing stories, laughing and joking. We talked about each other's up bringing and she was surprised when she found out that I dreamt of one day becoming a professional Boxer. After our long conversation, I went into my mom's room and took a bottle of vodka off her mini bar and placed it on my nightstand. Then I ran down the stairs taking two steps at a time, rushing to the kitchen to get two cans of tomato juice and two glasses. And like I took two steps at a time going down the stairs, I took two steps at a time running back up the stairs rushing back to Momo. When I reached my bedroom, she was already in the nude, undressed laying beneath my red silk sheets. Momo sat up revealing her beautiful African like statue breast. I poured her a Bloody Mary and she extended her hand and accepted the drink. I turned on the stereo and put on my Earth Wind and Fire and Isley Brother's mix tape. I took off my clothes and climbed into the bed with Mo. While Momo laid with her head on my chest, she started feeling guilty because she felt as though she was betraying Violet. But I explained to her that me and Violet would never be nothing more than friends. She just was a cool chick who deserved to be treated better. As the vodka took over, Momo became emotional about what happened between her and her boyfriend. She started revealing all her man's business. Mo's man was a major shot caller up in Harlem who wasn't too big on security. After Mo gave me the run down on this silly nigga, I made love to her like no other because I was rewarding her for that information. If I didn't learn anything else from that experience, I learned that if you ain't going to treat your chick right, she shouldn't know any of your business. Because pillow talk is a motherfucker and that's how I got the information for the lick that I put Pep on.

CHAPTER THIRTY

DIANA ROSS

After weeks of Pep sitting on dude up in Harlem, Pep finds out that he lives in Rochdale Queens and not in Harlem like we suspected. This made the job a whole lot easier because in Rochdale, there were quiet back streets away from the main Ave and intersections which were a stick-up kid's and a snatch boy's dream. This cat lived in a middleclass, working-class neighborhood which was ironic considering how loud and flamboyant his character was portrayed uptown in Harlem. After weeks of staking this cat out we acknowledged that this kid was a complete actor. The way he carried himself in Queens was totally contrary to the way he behaved up in Harlem. In Harlem he was your typical loudmouth, self-centered, flamboyant typical Alpo or Frank Lucas type if you know what I mean. He wasn't cut form the same material as Randy Love or Ivan or even Skip. Those three names were a different breed of Harlem niggas.

But nevertheless, this particular dude was a hustler if nothing else. He was caked up and in all honesty; he was rather bright because I sat in the car one day with Pep on one of his stakeouts and I was amazed at how this dude moved out in Queens. He carried himself like a total square and that shit alone required sheer brilliance but what he wasn't too smart about was, putting his hands on a vindictive female that had the pleasure of meeting mister cunning ass Unique.

On the morning of the robbery the sun illuminated the sky. Pep sat in his car waiting for dude's wife to leave for work. The plan was that once dude's wife left the house, dude would walk his mutt ass puppy to the store and then he would circle the block two or three times until his puppy took a shit. Then after his puppy relieved himself, he would then walk to the back of his house and open his garage. Inside of his garage he kept his organized gym set up. He had a weightlifting bench with multiple dumbbells, a pull up bar and a dip bar. In the middle of the spot there was a professional boxing heavy bag. Pep said, it was quite nice for one's personal use. Dude had no clue that while he went to take his punk ass puppy for a walk, Pep creeped into his backyard and hid, anticipating his return. Pep said he watched him come in through the driveway and chain the dog up to his fence. Once he chained the dog up, he then got on the ground and did some stretching exercises. Then out of nowhere, Pep said he ran in and made him strip down to some tight ass biker spandex body suit. He said dude had on some salt and pepper push it video type shit. Pep said he almost ruined the entire robbery because he was about to burst out laughing. As Pep told me the story, I was saying to myself typical Harlem nigga shit. Most of them niggas are secretly divas anyway. Not in a homo perspective, but more on an extreme metro sexual type of thing. Even down to their hand gestures, neck jerking and their sassy bragging mouth pieces. Pep told me that when dude jumped up on the pull up bar that's when he came out from behind the bushes displaying his gun. He said homeboy froze as if he seen a damn ghost. He said dude opened his mouth to scream but, nothing seemed to come out of his mouth. Pep told homeboy if he makes a sound, it would be the last sound that he would ever make. Pep then walked up on dude and bitch slapped the shit out of homeboy. Pep said when he slapped him, the dude said to him, please don't mess my face up. Please he repeated. Pep said he thought to himself, here it is I'm standing in front of this bitch ass nigga and all he's worrying about is his face getting messed up. Pep said he slapped him again and said bitch shut the fuck up! He said that once he a look at dude, he realized that homeboy was really a handsome dude and that he took pride in his looks. Pep said that he couldn't help but slap his ass again because he hated vain ass, soft niggas that should had been some type of model in the first place. Instead of being out in the streets, in the game, and taking up space for a real nigga. Dude was like 6'3 in height. Weighing maybe 180 pounds. His caramel complexion is probably what drove most broads crazy because his skin was totally flawless. This bitch ass nigga had almond shaped eyes and had the nerve to have them shaped up. Pep said this shit made him slap again just to hear him flinch up like the bitch he truly was. Plus, I told Pep what he did to Mo, and Pep was against men putting their paws on females, so he intended to bring the Dianna Ross out of dude. And Dianna Ross he brought out of this bitch made nigga.

Pep said after he finished tormenting dude, he grabbed home boy around the neck and made him enter the house through his back entrance. Once they were inside Pep made dude sit down at the kitchen table, and he sat across from him never taking his eyes or his gun off dude. He asked dude, where do you keep the money? Without wasting any time homeboy pointed to the large deep freezer. Pep said he stood up and motioned for ole boy to go to the deep freezer to get the money out and place it on the kitchen table. But before he allowed ole boy to got to the deep freezer, he said to him you don't have a gun in there now do you. Because I would hate to blow your motherfucking head off into that deep freezer. Homeboy says nah brother, I'm not playing any games. Pep says, I don't want to hear that brother black power shit. What are you trying to be funny or something? Then slapped him up against the back of his head and said just shut the fuck up and get what I came here for! He said that homeboy opened the deep freezer and dug inside and came up with a bag full of cold cash. Before grabbing the money, Pep pulled out a set of handcuffs and walked homeboy into his bathroom and hand cuffed him to the bathroom radiator and then spun around and walked outside and took the chained-up dog into the house and did some crazy abstract shit. He said he took duct taped the niggas punk ass dog to the dude's chest. All while laughing his ass off. He said the guy asked him, are you going to kill me? Pep didn't respond at first then he said the guy started crying and praying. Pep said he then slap the shit out of dude and told him, motherfucker I ain't going to kill your bitch ass but here's some advice, you need to get a bigger and meaner dog dude. As Pep was about to leave, he said homeboy had the nerve to ask who set him up? Pep turned back around and walked up on homeboy and bent down and in a low whisper, he asked dude, did he really want to know? Yes, I'll make it worth your while. Pep said, he acted as if he was interested and said oh really huh! Dude said, please let me know. Pep said he yelled out, "my dick!" And walked away laughing. Pep told us the story while we all sat in my mother's living room laughing our asses off. I lined the job up for Pep because he was a good dude, and I knew he would break my mom off lovely. Plus, I did it because I was kind of digging ole girl Mo and I wanted her to know she was my nigga, and I wouldn't tolerate nobody fucking with anybody who showed me care and concern. So, for a while my homie lover friend Momo was happy as hell everything turned out well. Everybody was happy. Mo even broke me off a couple of thousand.

EPILOGUE

In my last chapter I spoke briefly on the single female parent issue. Black women you are priceless! Father's Day was a non-existing factor in my life. The streets, the state penitentiary, mistakes and errors were my father. The only physical father I ever had just happened to be a female. My Momma! Again, black women you are priceless! Father's Day reflects sentiments of a child, whether male or female. Greeting their dads on such a beautiful day and showing some form of admiration, I assume but I wouldn't know. Father's Day, to me was a nightmare. The acknowledgement of not being loved or wanted. That shit to me was only a dream because I wasn't blessed to have a Dad. Do you know how many people like myself grow up fucked up in the head because daddy isn't around? Unfortunately, a whole lot. Shit there are a lot of instances where the father's absence contributes to young kids broken dreams. Lonely moments, sitting somewhere in a funky ass apartment staring out of a window waiting for his or her dad to show up. Waiting for the nigga to show up to graduations, or a boxing event. Hoping to see their dad cheering them the on. Man, if that ain't some painful shit, then I don't know what pain is! But we're supposed to work diligently to change the narrative and stop repeating cycles of our past. It is a must that we stand erect as men!

SHOUT OUT TO ALL MY GHETTO BASTARDS

www.ingramcontent.com/pod-product-compliance
Lightning Source LLC
Chambersburg PA
CBHW022101150426
43195CB00008B/221